People Pleasing

Practical Guidance to Fix Your Codependency and Stop Being a People Pleasing

(How to Start Saying No Set Healthy Boundaries and Express Yourself)

Kerry Black

Published By **Phil Dawson**

Kerry Black

All Rights Reserved

People Pleasing: Practical Guidance to Fix Your Codependency and Stop Being a People Pleasing (How to Start Saying No Set Healthy Boundaries and Express Yourself)

ISBN 978-1-7388267-9-7

No part of this guidebook shall be reproduced in any form without permission in writing from the publisher except in the case of brief quotations embodied in critical articles or reviews.

Legal & Disclaimer

The information contained in this ebook is not designed to replace or take the place of any form of medicine or professional medical advice. The information in this ebook has been provided for educational & entertainment purposes only.

The information contained in this book has been compiled from sources deemed reliable, and it is accurate to the best of the Author's knowledge; however, the Author cannot guarantee its accuracy and validity and cannot be held liable for any errors or omissions. Changes are periodically made to this book. You must consult your doctor or get professional medical advice before using any of the suggested remedies, techniques, or information in this book.

Upon using the information contained in this book, you agree to hold harmless the Author from and against any damages, costs, and expenses, including any legal fees potentially resulting from the application of any of the information provided by this guide. This disclaimer applies to any damages or injury caused by the use and application, whether directly or indirectly, of any advice or information presented, whether for breach of contract, tort, negligence, personal injury, criminal intent, or under any other cause of action.

You agree to accept all risks of using the information presented inside this book. You need to consult a professional medical practitioner in order to ensure you are both able and healthy enough to participate in this program.

Table Of Contents

Chapter 1: People Pleasing 101–The Signs And Symptoms 1

Chapter 2: Step #1: Build An Intention And Find Your Compelling Whys 14

Chapter 3: Step #2: Be Aware Of Yourself And Your Emotions 29

Chapter 4: Step #3: Accept Yourself And Your Emotions 40

Chapter 5: Boost Your Self-Confidence .. 73

Chapter 6: Please Stop Pleasing 86

Chapter 7: No Is Your Biggest Weapon 116

Chapter 8: The Buck Stops Here 139

Chapter 1: People Pleasing 101–The Signs And Symptoms

"If you don't turn your lifestyles proper proper into a tale, you clearly become a part of a person else's tale.'

Terry Pratchet

Turning your existence into a story does not suggest you need to hitchhike your way to the Bahamas or embark on a solo Mount Everest mountain climbing journey. No, you don't want to do something amazing-unstable or adventurous to expose your life right right into a personal tale.

Turning your lifestyles into a tale manner you need to emerge as the protagonist for your lifestyles. It calls on you to forestall living the existence of a assisting character, or worse, a sidekick.

No way to Hollywood movies, being a deuteragonist, a sidekick, sounds glamorous: it's no longer as it places you in a characteristic in which the whole lot about your existence facilitates the principle person's story. That's no longer a high-quality manner to live lifestyles! The extremely good lifestyles is in which your tale is ready you, not someone else.

Unfortunately, writing your tale can be difficult to accomplish in case you are a human beings pleaser.

To assist you recognize how being a human beings pleaser sabotages your existence and why you have to overcome this problem, permit's speak a number of the superb signs and signs and symptoms that illustrate people-beautiful inclinations:

Am I A People Pleaser: How to Tell (Signs)

We all find it irresistible even as unique human beings appreciate and are glad with us. Since we (humans) have an innate want to socialise, bond with, and enjoy related to others, we regularly appearance after cherished ones' wishes to gather care and appreciation from them in move again.

While there's no longer something incorrect with that, it's honestly virtually worth noting that there's a difference among being concerned for others and going overboard with lovely them.

The former includes adopting a type mind-set toward others, looking after their goals while putting healthful limitations that make sure exceptional humans behave respectfully with you.

On the other hand, the latter refers to the tendency to adopt the area of caretaker to the quantity which you live, breathe, and flow into round for others, great all their requests at the detriment of having any existence left to stay for yourself. Being in such a function may be very toxic on your nicely-being.

If you remember you studied you're a humans pleaser but aren't one hundred% positive, proper here're the behavioral signs and symptoms and signs and symptoms and signs to look out for for your demeanor:

#1: You seem to don't forget virtually every body spherical you

It's perfect to pay attention civilly to unique evaluations and be respectful of them; doing that lets in you come backpedal as a reverent and accepting individual.

However, that does not advocate you want to accept as actual with truly anyone handiest because you are too scared to refuse some component or due to the truth you want distinctive people to love you all of the time.

If you find out your self nodding your head to the whole lot your associate says or, notwithstanding the truth which you disagree with them, agreeing along side your friends' viewpoints handiest because you don't need to make your buddies glad, you've got got human beings-captivating inclinations.

#2: You take responsibility for unique peoples' emotions

Building meaningful private and professional relations calls for growing your emotional intelligence (EI.) Emotional intelligence consists of know-how your and extraordinary peoples' feelings and successfully managing every to preserve jointly useful relationship conditions.

It's exquisite if you realize how your behavior influences others and may stay calm while others round you're seething with anger, maintaining the scenario now not exacerbating.

However, if you keep in mind you are accountable for how others revel in, which causes you to live silent whilst human beings are imply to you, you want to apprehend that everybody is accountable for how they experience.

Moreover, being responsible for the feelings of the humans round you isn't healthful; it's a extreme, humans-fascinating conduct that dreams immediate addressing.

#3: You apologize hundreds even whilst you're no longer wrong

Do you discover your self saying 'sorry' to others in spite of the reality that they have got wronged you? Do you blame your self for the whole lot that is going incorrect for your circle of relatives' existence?

Well, if you do, recognize that:

Frequently apologizing for the mess other humans make is an indication of low self-esteem. It indicates your lack of confidence and your decided want for outdoor validations, each of which may be unconducive on your properly-being.

#4: Other human beings bombard you with their requests

You awaken and accumulate a message out of your buddy asking you to artwork on his venture. A few hours later, your cousin drops thru and goals you to help her create her website. When you meet your friends inside the night time, you get maintain of requests to run some errands for them.

Every day, you've got thousands of things to do, most of which is probably for one of a kind human beings and unrelated for your desires and goals. The truth which you are usually working for others shows you're a humans pleaser.

#five: You are afraid to say no to others

If you nearly choke out on every occasion you have to say 'no' to someone asking for a need and feature ever refuse peoples' requests although while it's almost no longer viable for you, it shows you cannot stand up to your rights.

Whether you fear human beings will start hating you, otherwise you lack the courage to reject a person's dreams, you cannot utter a 'no' out of your mouth. That even hurts you from internal due to the fact you continuously find yourself immersed in piles of duties thrown at you with the beneficial aid of others.

#6: You can't stand having someone dissatisfied with you

When you see a person frown at you or pull away whilst he/she sees you coming close to, it hurts you deeply. You come to be very uncomfortable whilst humans are dissatisfied with you due to the fact you can not stand that idea. So a protracted way, you've got were given incredible lived your existence for others, that is why you can't digest the fact that people can be angry with you.

Moreover, if a person is mad at you, you blame yourself for it and go overboard with candy-speaking the person. Since you can't undergo the sight of a person being aggravated with you, you bypass the extra mile to be appeasing.

#7: You behave superficially

Although one-of-a-kind human beings perform specific elements of our person, when you have a bent to behave greater like the ones round you and undertake a superficial demeanor to delight others, you're deep within the trenches of humans-captivating.

If you normally begin acting snobbish at the same time as a terrific-wealthy and haughty friend drops through or behave like an highbrow and forestall cracking lame jokes—

your conventional self—at the same time as your cousin who teaches at Stanford visits, you interact in those behaviors to delight others.

You want to recognize the significance of being your self and how being snug to your pores and pores and skin will carry out the actual you, giving human beings a risk to love that man or woman.

Unfortunately, if you're a people-pleaser, you'll struggle with this reality and could keep your fake conduct, hoping to obtain love from others.

#eight: You crave reward to revel in glad

Sweet terms of appreciation cheer us up. However, if your emotional contentment is based upon on the sort phrases and reward exclusive human beings give you, it's probable which you're counting on their validation to happiness.

If people you like and care approximately don't reward you, you enjoy deeply saddened after which resort to particular measures to thrill them handiest to concentrate 'You are lovable' or 'I love you' from them.

When you are not around people, searching after their wishes, you revel in lonely due to the fact searching after others is what you understand the manner to do. Since you in no way have interaction in sports activities that bring you happiness, you don't recognize a manner to be glad with youself, nor do you have interaction in topics that convey you pleasure.

#9: You keep away from battle

It is good to be peaceful and warfare-unfastened however heading off conflict in any respect charges, even though human beings deny your rights, suggests that you war to rise up for yourself. You frequently allow yourself incur the wrath of others excellent to avoid experiencing any war.

If you always keep away from battle because of the truth you lack the courage to fight for your rights, don't need to harm others, or strength others away, you need to begin strolling on this hassle.

#10: You in no way take shipping of your emotions of being damage

It is vital to definitely be given and consist of your feelings, collectively with being harm, unhappy, angry, jealous, and scared. However, in case you're frequently fearful of displeasing precise people, you in all likelihood in no manner admit while you revel in pained or while others disappoint you.

You are so used to feeling wounded from inner which you allow yourself cry on my own with out sharing your feelings with every person.

#eleven: You secretly preference you could do the assets you need to do

Do you regularly want that a fantastic buddy would possibly save you displaying up due to the fact you don't like spending time with him/her at his/her desired restaurant?

Do you secretly pray that your bossy colleague will leave work early so you can sit down down in a cubicle of your choice?

If you could relate to those situations, you may be a people-fascinating pushover who's invisible to others.

Secretly, you wish that first-class conditions may additionally occur, imparting you with a threat to do belongings you need to do due to the reality you lack the self assurance to do what your coronary coronary heart wills.

The idea of frightening others and no longer receiving appreciation is quite a large scare and deterrent that continues you doing what others want from you in preference to what you in reality want to do. That is why you extremely good secretly desire for assets you want however in no way clearly pursue or gather them.

Since you currently apprehend those eleven humans-lovely signs and symptoms and signs and symptoms, start searching at your self for them.

If you regularly phrase a couple of these elements for your persona of conduct and constantly discover yourself at one-of-a-type peoples' ordinary beck and speak to, it's substantially stable to finish which you're a human beings pleaser, and need to art work on overcoming this behavior.

Let's flow into to the following financial ruin wherein we'll start discussing the first step you can use to get started out on turning into greater self-assured and steady enough to prevent being a pushover:

Chapter 2: Step #1: Build An Intention And Find Your Compelling Whys

Renowned truth seeker Seneca as quickly as stated, "Not how prolonged, however how well you have got lived is the principle problem."

In most things, first-rate trumps amount. Likewise, almost approximately the way you live your life, great trumps quantity. While how lengthy you have got were given lived subjects to you, you also need to stay a fulfilling and empowering existence.

That does now not honestly want to be a dream.

You can watch movies for a residing, begin your Vlog regardless of the fact that humans disagree with the concept, and grow to be a fashion fashion designer notwithstanding the truth that your controlling dad disapproves of it.

You can do all that and plenty greater and infuse herbal pleasure, harmony, and this means that into your existence with the aid of assuming command of it. The first step to do this is to set the right purpose for it.

How to Set an Unwavering Intention to Stop Being a People Pleaser

It is critical to devote yourself to any reason you revel in driven to gain; handiest then are you able to stick with it and actualize it for real.

Now which you have explored your behavior in element and diagnosed the numerous human beings-desirable symptoms and symptoms and signs and symptoms you display, you could get started out on the technique of overcoming this, step certainly one of that is to create an purpose to overcome the hassle for appropriate.

Intention includes accepting the hassle and setting forward your desire to cope with the difficulty for suitable. It is important to solidify your willpower through writing it down in order that whenever you study it, you bear in mind your intention and maintain on with it but the chances stacked in competition to you.

When you do not forget your cause and goal severally, you can pull yourself thru the bootstraps, get again on the right tune, and maintain pursuing your dreams until you ultimately gather it—in this situation, overcoming the tendency to pleasure human beings, becoming a pushover within the technique.

Here're numerous strategic strategies you could use to create your motive to accomplish that:

#: Accept the problem

First:

You want to verbally acquire your codependency on others for validation and happiness and your tendency to great appearance after considered one of a kind humans's nicely-being.

This recognition can be overwhelming; it may bring decrease again some painful recollections of the manner others mistreated you at the identical time as you went above and past to help them out.

It is k. Life is hard at instances, however it does no longer ought to be this way, and it in reality will decorate at the identical time as you start searching after yourself higher. You can try this!

Here's the way to art work all the way down to self-popularity

• Take a deep breath, and take a few other extra.

• Inhale via your nostril to a depend of four and exhale through your mouth to a count number wide variety of 6. Engage in this workout for a few moments.

• When you sense calmer, say a few detail calming at the side of, 'This too shall bypass' or 'It is k, I enjoy all right.'

• Reflect on the behavioral signs of being a humans pleaser that you positioned in yourself.

• Think of the way you've got have been given been nurturing others all of your life and the way you have allowed one-of-a-kind people to cope with you need an invisible caregiver.

• In that light, take transport of that you are a human beings pleaser and desire to paintings on that area by way of way of saying something along facet, 'I am a humans pleaser and ñow running to overcome the trouble to be happier and greater wholesome.' Saying that is you accepting the trouble—it's life.

• At this aspect, strive now not to be judgmental of yourself due to the reality if you act harshly with your self, you're possibly to enjoy extra damage. You may additionally moreover experience feelings of unhappiness or maybe anger constructing up internal you while you famend your people-captivating conduct. At that factor, maintain breathing deeply to calm your self down and glaringly reduce the emotions of harm, unhappiness, and frustration.

To be given your present day nature and increase your motivation to paintings on it, practice this exercising numerous instances each day:

#: Create your purpose

Once you get to some extent in that you experience which you've embraced the problem absolutely, you presently need to transport within the route of resolving it, which starts offevolved with placing your intention.

Here's what you need to do:

• Now you need to craft your willpower to art work to your shortcoming so you can live a better lifestyles. You may additionally want to say and write some factor in conjunction with,

o "I am actively working on my tendency to thrill others in order that I experience unfastened, satisfied, and emotionally solid" or,

o "I am overcoming my humans-appealing inclinations to be happier and enjoy greater wholesome."

• Please write down this—and every other such assertion you provide you with—in a magazine committed in your journey in the direction of becoming robust, happy, and impartial from the want to are attempting to find out of doors validation in your happiness.

• Go via this aim each morning, say it out loud as you take a look at it, and then write it 3 instances once more on a today's web internet web page. Doing this may embed the belief to your unconscious mind. This exercising rewires your thoughts to think certainly, consciousness to your goal, and take tremendous motion to free up yourself of this behavior for appropriate.

• . Jokes aside, it's far a beneficial gadget that ensures you don't neglect something essential. It labels information "important" and "unimportant" to you with the aid of reading how frequently you bear in mind it. When you continuously undergo your purpose to prevent being a humans pleaser and be happier as an person, it embraces the idea as in my view giant. The immediately it places some statistics in the 'crucial' magnificence, it shifts your interest to facts, motivating you to take active movement to beautify that location. When you chant your reason to control your people-best inclinations, you continuously remind yourself of your dedication, spark off your RAS, and make it artwork actively to help you objectify that motive. ☐Reticular Activating System (RAS) is a tool on your mind that filters out pointless and saves critical information to prevent an facts overload—otherwise, your thoughts might also moreover explode

Now that you have created your goal, solidified it, and activated your RAS in the path of it, the subsequent step is to dig out your compelling whys to paste to this purpose.

How to Find Your Compelling Whys

Self-help guru Antony Robbins is an propose of locating your compelling whys as a way to ensure you live committed to accomplishing a particular purpose.

Your compelling whys linked to any willpower are the motives why you choice to gain it. They are all the factors and reasons why you cannot make do with out the aim and why you experience that you should accomplish it at any rate.

Let's face it, as you determine toward a specific purpose, say, dropping 20 pounds, developing your productivity at artwork, or now not being a human beings pleaser anymore, as is the case on this modern-day scenario, you may come upon a few barriers.

There may be instances at the same time as you could now not need to art work closer to your willpower, instances at the same time as you'll stumble upon barriers so bold that all you want to do is end, and times whilst your motivation can be no longer anything but fumes.

While such times are difficult, you need to strength thru them to make it to the quit line.

That is wherein your compelling whys are to be had accessible. Your whys refuel your motivation thru reminding you of why you location effective desires within the first place and why you must take a look at via irrespective of what comes your manner.

Your 'whys' basically create a hunger to your cause and stress you inside the course of them. Like Les Brown, a renowned motivational speaker, as quickly as stated,

"Wanting a few issue isn't enough. You should have a hunger for it. Your motivation need to be in reality compelling in order to overcome the barriers as a way to perpetually come your manner."

Now which you recognize you want to save you being a humans pleaser without a doubt so people appreciate you, save you treating you need an invisible caregiver, and you start feeling happier, you want to find out your compelling whys.

Here is how you may do this:

- Sit someplace peaceful and quiet collectively at the side of your magazine in hand so you can anticipate lightly.

- Think of the manner being a humans pleaser has negatively impacted your existence.

- Recall the instances at the same time as humans mistreated you despite the fact that you've got got generally helped them out. Recall the times at the same time as no individual prioritized your properly-being and did matters that made you sad, but you chose to just accept their alternatives. Think of even as you desired to pursue your goals but could not due to the fact you feared scary the authority figures on your lifestyles. Recall how no individual asks you the manner you experience or what you want; all they do is bombard you with wishes, requests, and directives. Think of the way you are continuously searching for validation from others to be glad and joyous, and the way because of this you stay your lifestyles for unique humans.

- Build on those reasons, and write particular money owed related to them so you get a clearer picture of the way captivating others is ruining your existence.

• After reading a majority of those frightening information, picture how calm, non violent, and enormous a life you shall live while you forestall overcaring for others.

• Think of methods, even as you prevent going for walks errands for others day in and time out, you'll have time to artwork on your weblog, interact in gardening, and do volunteer paintings with safe haven houses, as you have got constantly favored to do. Now think of the manner you acquired't should experience harm even as human beings refuse you for a few factor no matter the fact that you exit of your manner to assist them. Think of the way you may start living for yourself, locate time to your wishes, and pursue your passions.

• Reflect on how self-assured and emotionally steady you'll enjoy and come to be while you overcome the need to pride others and are looking for their validation. Naturally, at the identical time as you're not pinning after your associate's approval and might make choices for your very very very own, you revel in extra confident. Moreover, whilst you aren't associating your happiness with external elements like specific people, you discover ways to be glad from being who you're and doing matters that remember to you.

• Picture how non violent existence shall become whilst you in the long run make particular powerful improvements for your lifestyles and start feeling cushty for your pores and skin due to the fact you wouldn't care masses approximately what others consider you or how they want you to stay.

• Jot down those motives for your journal so that you can replicate on them and file them.

• Go thru those reasons at least as quickly as every day clearly so the reasons why you ought to live for your self, not for others, grow to be extra evident.

• Take a few put up-its and write down your compelling motives following the examples verified underneath. Paste the ones publish-

its at specific locations of your private home which you frequently float beyond in order that every time you walk past them, you get mild reminders of why you need to surrender your addiction of fascinating human beings.

o Living for myself makes me experience happier.

o Overcoming my need to satisfaction others brings freedom and peace of thoughts.

o I in reality have extra time to artwork on my duties.

o I sense confident once I make my private alternatives.

o I sense cushty in my skin.

o I am the boss of my life.

o I do what my coronary coronary heart wills.

o I rise up for my rights.

o I locate it smooth to voice my mind.

• Such slight reminders and distinctive debts of your compelling whys will instill in you a sturdy choice to triumph over your human beings-cute behavior.

Now which you are through with the crucial step of accepting your hassle, intending to paintings on it, and finding the motives to satisfy your commitment, you can bypass up the device ladder to the subsequent step, which revolves round self-popularity and self-reputation.

Chapter 3: Step #2: Be Aware Of Yourself And Your Emotions

Self-awareness and self-reputation are the golden keys to unlocking your excellent life and being authentically yourself.

A giant cause why lots of us are humans pleasers is that we need to benefit appreciation and acknowledgment, some component rooted in a lack of validation from our internal selves.

When we fail to just accept ourselves as we are, we will be inclined to look up to people for validation to be ok with ourselves. Moreover, while we don't apprehend who we are or what we need, we commonly have a tendency to accept some element others determine is good for us. Even regardless of the fact that we may also agree to that, deep down, it creates an internal resentment.

For example:

You can also observe take a look at electric powered engineering due to the reality your father has decided that's what's superb for you, but you aren't glad with the selection. However, because you don't recognize what precisely you want, you lack the braveness and any logical cause to oppose his choice.

Moreover, in case you suppose you aren't particular at deciding topics for yourself, you could find it much less complicated to surrender to his whims in vicinity of exploring what your coronary heart clearly desires.

To in the long run forestall charming others and upward push up for your self, one of the important things you can not get past is the importance of gaining reputation of who you authentically are, what you virtually want, and acquire yourself lovingly.

You can use those techniques to carry out that:

#: Become More Self Aware

Self-interest refers to spending time with yourself out of the aim of exploring terrific elements of your individual higher, statistics your thoughts and emotions, and turning into greater privy to your real desires so you prevent pursuing superficial dreams.

When you invite your emotions and mind into a rustic of nonjudgmental cognizance, it allows you to recognize and examine from them in area of most effective reacting to them.

You assemble interest of your truth through becoming open to the concept of encountering your truths. This process is a completely possible, powerful device that assist you to understand the reasons inside the lower back of your humans-attractive behavior so that you can pick out the foundation reason and nip it inside the bud.

For example, you may recognize which you please others due to the reality you're a in reality compassionate individual who can't say 'no' to human beings. In that case, you'll understand that one of the assets you need to do is have a look at and hold close the art work of putting limitations that can help you stay an emotionally strong and extra healthful lifestyles.

Similarly, you could first-rate grow to be passionate enough to pursue your ambition for pictures in region of studying advertising as your controlling older brother needs if you understand that ardour exists, which can great take vicinity if you spend time with your self.

Here is how you could start getting self-awareness and statistics yourself better:

• Every day, create a 10-30 minute reflected photo window for self-pondered photo to your mind and desires.

• Ask your self approximately what you need the most, and what brings you herbal pride. Please write down the solutions, after which mirror on whether or not that's what you need honestly or if it's every different choice you absorbed from someone else.

• Think of why you warfare with announcing 'no' to humans and why you work so hard to preserve them happy. Use the 'why' approach to parent out your root motive of becoming a human beings pleaser. Ask your self, "Why do I please others?" If the answer is, "So that they decide on me," ask your self the why query: "Why do I want humans to like me?" Keep digging into it, asking your self why topics are a great way till you get to the lowest of the actual hassle.

• Write down the awesome root motives behind your humans-attractive behavior that you could recognize from this practice. In the chapters that observe, we'll communicate a manner to cope with root troubles.

• Also, please spend some time reflecting on what you choice to do in lifestyles and the higher techniques in which you want to apply a while. Reflect in your likes, dislikes, interests, hobbies, passions, and interests so you can create a listing of factors you need to interact in with the time you'll now must your self.

• Make pleasant you write down the entirety so you can without problem undergo those findings and recognize yourself higher.

Self-popularity is an ongoing adventure that never completely stops, but you need to begin it to understand the real you. As you slowly discover and apprehend yourself, you get clarity on whom you authentically are and become stimulated to prioritize your needs. This recognition is so powerful that it allow you to overcome your want to pride others.

#: Become privy to your feelings

While running on information your mind, you furthermore may need to gain a higher recognition of your feelings.

Our emotions have an effect on our thoughts, actions, and selections. You sense glad at the same time as your buddy praises you, and in go lower back, you agree to work on their thesis without getting any remuneration in alternate. You revel in unhappy even as your mother and father appear to expose more affection to your sibling, and because of that, you try to please them to get the same treatment.

Different feelings, which embody happiness, disappointment, anger, envy, and fear, have an impact on us otherwise. They make us behave in procedures that now and again we don't even want to interact in in any respect.

You might not want to go the more mile for a egocentric character, but you continue to do as he/she dreams because of the truth come what can also, your unhappiness compels you to have a friend round, and simply so that you don't lose that pal, you compromise to do the entirety he/she goals.

When we start cultivating better emotional popularity, we're able to apprehend awesome feelings and the manner they have an effect on our attitudes and picks. Moreover, emotional reputation offers perception into how being handled as a pushover makes you experience, helping you recognize how doing too much hurts you deeply.

By being emotionally self-aware, you understand that inter-courting nicely-being and prosperity depend on the manner you behave with others and, more importantly, the manner you address your self.

If you're generally available at anyone else's disposal, you end up doing an excessive amount of for them and over-feature in all of your relationships. That continuously leads the opportunity people to "beneath-function" and one manner or the opportunity damage you in the approach. People might not intend to hurt you, but because of the fact you are normally over-functioning, they start to forget approximately their obligations and cope with you as a pushover.

To end this tendency, you need to understand your emotions better, what triggers them, after which use that recognition to save you human beings-lovely all the time so that you can deal with your desires for a alternate.

Here is what you want to do now:

• Reflect on why you enjoy sad or depressed in lifestyles and what triggers those feelings. If you're disenchanted at how nobody offers you importance of their existence, reflect on how that each one started out. Maybe you began out going out of your manner to useful useful resource others, which by a few method made them "under-feature" and burden you with their part of the inter-relation equation.

• Please additionally undergo in thoughts how indignant you experience due to the truth humans don't recognize you or address you with the consideration and kindness you deserve. If you're sincere, you'll probable have a look at that this boils down to the reality that you in no way set any obstacles for your relationships.

• Moreover, consider how you react on your feelings of satisfaction on every occasion someone praises you or fortunately proclaims how you're usually being worried for them. Maybe, it's far the ones feelings of brief happiness and success that compel you to delight others. While this happiness offers you a few pride, acquire that it's fleeting and does now not yield lasting internal contentment.

• The extra you mirror in your emotions, the better you'll recognize the manner you allow others to mistreat you and how you continuously have energy and desire in your existence. If you allow human beings maltreat you, it's because of the truth you've given away your power and desire by using now not putting boundaries; you've made yourself available to their beck and get in touch with. Once you recognize you've got have been given a preference, you will be in a role to reveal your entire life spherical for the higher.

• Ensure that you write the whole thing down on your mag and mirror on those findings; that manner, you may take better steering from your feelings.

All the ones findings will help you slowly triumph over your tendency to pleasure one among a kind people in desire to your self, in case you want to will let you allow pass of the addiction and come to be the real boss of your lifestyles.

In addition to being aware about your self, you furthermore may want to sincerely accept your self and your emotions. Let us discover this problem higher within the following financial disaster.

Chapter 4: Step #3: Accept Yourself And Your Emotions

Now which you have taken a step toward becoming greater privy to your mind, emotions, and real goals, the subsequent critical step to use that cognizance to your self and take delivery of the actual you. Like environmentalist Dr. Bill Jackson says, "To discover the pleasant lifestyles, you want to come to be yourself."

Only thru accepting your self are you able to gain the braveness to unfastened up your proper self, unfold your wings some distance and large, prepared to take your flight in the international.

You may not be aware about this proper now, but a high-quality motive why humans deal with you as a pushover is which you don't exhibit your proper persona. You don't stand for your rights, by no means dare to unique your opinion, and never allow your proper slight to shine. Naturally, whilst no one is privy to the actual you, no person will revel in interested in the real you.

Since you've devoted to self-betterment, allow's talk why and the manner to take shipping of yourself and your feelings.

Why You Need to Accept Yourself Wholeheartedly (and How)

Finally, you want to begin going for walks on accepting and loving your actual and proper self.

Because you're now extra self-aware and apprehend your feelings higher, you may use that realize-a manner to peek deeper into yourself to decide out your actual self.

People pleasers have a addiction of being superficial in the front of those they want to please; it's a method they use to advantage approval. You likely do the equal.

Maybe you laugh out too loud in the front of your noisy, boisterous pals after they crack lame jokes approximately you so that they don't prevent spending time with you even though you don't discover them highbrow sufficient.

Maybe you play golfing collectively together with your boss, no matter the fact which you despise the sport and prefer playing basketball simply so he/she maintains considering you for a merchandising.

Acting in methods that please others provides transitory satisfaction, however have you ever ever ever belief approximately how that makes you enjoy approximately your self? It is possibly you draw back at these superficial acts and need to change them for ideal.

Now that you need to stay lifestyles on your terms, why now not do that for real? To do that, you first want to come to phrases with your self and lovingly receive your self with open arms.

Being your authentic self isn't a few element you need to compromise due to the fact at the same time as you are your actual self, you recognize who you're from internal and might assemble a meaningful lifestyles for yourself.

For instance, on the equal time as you receive that you are a deep highbrow, you can stop spending time with folks that don't hobby you and discover realistic pals with whom to spend time. Maybe in case you start playing basketball greater, you may make a outstanding friend or two and create your "tribe."

Moreover, the pride that comes from proudly proudly owning your character is unrivaled:

When you act authentically, you start respecting yourself, and whilst you appreciate yourself, special people feel that and respect you in turn. You may be capable of get a few words of appreciation from those you attempt to imitate, but it's far probably those human beings chuckle at you in the again of your decrease again for being phony.

To be surely you and revel in cushty to your pores and skin, please start accepting yourself instead of looking for to borrow "skins from different humans" or forcefully looking for to in shape within the ones coverings.

Moreover, while you're taking shipping of yourself, you include all of your strengths and weaknesses, essential to self-improvement without any self-sabotaging behaviors. You perceive your shortcomings, improve them, and become a complicated model of your self with out bashing yourself. Naturally, whilst you emerge as better, you want yourself higher and draw people's attention.

If you want to live a happy lifestyles without in search of to be a person you aren't, you need to simply accept yourself.

Here're sensible guidelines you can use to artwork towards that:

#: Describe your actual self

With your magazine with the beneficial aid of your thing, sit down somewhere in which you enjoy calm so you can peacefully recollect your self. Think of who you are, your individual inclinations, and what describes you wonderful.

If you are compelled about your character now, consider the way you behaved and lived as a kid. What matters did human beings praise you for or factor out approximately you? What had been your first rate man or woman traits, and what did you spend most of some time doing?

Also, please consider the way you experience about those around you and whether or no longer the urge to attend to others is real or a few aspect you do to benefit interest?

Write down those varieties of answers, one at a time, in your mag and reflect on them. It is okay if topics don't make lots enjoy to you before everything. You really want to hold exploring your self, reflecting on who you are, and jotting down the findings.

Go via the money owed multiple instances to set up a dating amongst top notch findings and discover your actual self.

#: Know your key strengths and weaknesses

When you explore yourself, you will in all likelihood come across a few or a whole lot of your strengths and weaknesses. Describe them in element and reflect onconsideration on how they have got an impact for your life.

If you are a being worried individual, how has that affected your existence? If you have got got a horrible dependancy of suppressing your feelings, how does which have an effect to your existence? If you revel in unconfident, how has that recommended your fact?

Jot the whole thing down, and turn out to be privy to five of your biggest strengths and weaknesses—5 for every. With each strength and susceptible point, write down its significance on your lifestyles and the manner it relates on your human beings-acceptable behavior.

#: Think about how human beings describe you

Also, think about how those round you describe and enjoy approximately you. Some humans dare to mention the meanest topics on your face, on the equal time as others are discreet approximately it and express their feelings via gestures and facial expressions.

If humans cope with you as a pushover, a number of them can be outrageous enough to name you hurtful names, and some can also furthermore shrug once they see you or laugh loudly at your errors.

While it may be painful to bear in mind such occurrences, endure in mind them severally—or a couple of times—so that you can recognize how people mistreat you and the way they recognize you.

Having this hobby moves you to an emotional point of view in which you can in the long run stand in your rights and stop being concerned too much for others. It moreover enables you recognize how others apprehend you, which offers you a deeper information of your individual.

You might also additionally understand that human beings frequently understand you as a silly man or woman who doesn't apprehend masses. However, in truth, you're a philosophical and mature individual who acts stupid to alter to sure social situations. If people don't understand you for trying to be more like them, why now not be extra like your actual self?

#: Accept who you're

Once you have got were given deeply contemplated on your self and are clearer on your real individual, it is time to start being more accepting towards yourself.

Here are a few methods to transport approximately this course:

• First, you want to install writing down who you truely are in a few sentences. Describe your extraordinary individual trends, and if maximum of them experience like shortcomings, be for the reason that too. If you're sloppy, type, underneath-confident, and timid, permit or not it's and describe your self the use of the high-quality adjectives that healthful your character.

• Next, say, "I take delivery of myself wholeheartedly and in reality, and revel in snug in my pores and pores and skin." This statement is an example of a wonderful confirmation. An affirmation is an offer you accept as true with in, and at the same time as you again and again chant some component or recognition on it, your subconscious accepts it as your reality and shifts your consciousness on that. Chanting a first rate affirmation rewires your thoughts to suppose clearly, helping you're making great modifications on your life and flow into in the course of development. Practice this specific affirmation or comparable ones again and again inside the path of the day so you continuously stimulate your thoughts to without a doubt take transport of yourself as you are.

• Every time you find out your self being harsh with your self, say, "I take delivery of myself, and I'm becoming higher." For instance, in case you made a mistake in an e mail you sent to a customer, don't bash yourself. Instead, deliver that patron each other email accepting your mistake to rectify it.

• Talk kindly with your self continually. Every time you are making a mistake or allow someone disrespect you, don't criticize your self. Instead, please comfort yourself thru pronouncing sweet things like, "It is okay. I am mastering to artwork on this problem and feeling higher already." Such tips help you form a first rate mind-set and be compassionate towards your self. Naturally, on the identical time as you exercising self-kindness, you find out it smooth to accept and be your self.

• Being your actual self is an integral part of self-reputation. Yes, this takes some time to stand up, however you want to start doing it right now. Since you presently have higher readability on who you are as a person, start expressing that too. If you're dramatic and prefer to infuse a few drama on your normal conversations, go with the flow in advance and do that. If you love analyzing poetry and are although a big Shakespeare fan, begin re-reading his works. You may additionally moreover have given up on that after your associate constantly made a laugh of your love for Shakespeare, but now which you have devoted to being greater self-accepting and right, there is no disgrace in professing your love for the maestro of English literature. Start taking little steps toward being who you are, so you slowly benefit greater braveness to set free your real self.

As you determine on those areas, you will phrase a marked development for your vanity and self perception stages. You will begin to price yourself more and experience your organisation m0re.

One manner to make certain which you maintain making progress is to provide the same understand and reputation to your emotions; anyhow, they will be an vital part of your character.

#: Build an accepting thoughts-set in the course of your emotions

Earlier, we mentioned the way to discover your feelings. This technique builds on that thru assisting you come to be greater accepting of them. A key cause in the decrease lower back of your people-captivating inclinations is your lack of emotional self-elegance.

Since others normally mistreat you and deny you the due apprehend and care you deserve, you probable have loads of pent-up frustration and ache effervescent inner you. Unlike maximum individuals who react on your emotions violently, you in all likelihood have a addiction of bottling up your emotions and channelizing them thru over-functioning for individuals who don't deal with you properly.

Instead of rejecting your emotions and suppressing them, now you want to turn out to be compassionate and accepting towards them. If you experience angry, damage, upset, sad, or jealous, explicit your feelings in reality in place of repressing them, and as a surrender result, feeling stifled.

Here is what you need to start doing greater frequently:

- Whenever someone saddens, hurts, or annoys you, sit lightly in conjunction with your emotion.

- Instead of distracting yourself from that emotion or doing some thing to please that man or woman who truely hurt you, have a examine your emotion so you can understand what it's looking to speak to you.

- If someone stated a few trouble advocate and hurtful to you, it's miles natural to revel in harm through it. Explore your sadness and recognize that the emotion shows you don't recognize such treatment. If you experience irritated that your pal ditched you for the umpteenth time at the same time as he/she promised to satisfy you and rather went out with someone else, a few element you recognize because of the Instagram memories, get hold of your anger as an emotional response to being ditched. Understand that you don't deserve this form of remedy, and you experience disillusioned through it.

• Write down the emotions your emotions stir internal you, and the remarkable emotions you enjoy in a single-of-a-type conditions.

• While you're sitting in conjunction with your emotion, keep away from shunning it; allow it out peacefully. To do that, permit your anger or sadness to upward thrust after which subside sizable at its personal tempo. The average timespan of feelings isn't longer than 12 mins. Thus, if you supply your self handiest 12 minutes, your anger, envy, unhappiness, and frustration will in reality lower and soothe.

• Once the emotion has calmed down, replicate all another time on what it have become on the lookout for to talk to you, and write down your emotions.

• Next, think of the manner to reply to the emotion calmly. We often most effective react to our emotions and superb conditions we come across. For example, on the equal time as we enjoy angered with the useful resource of a few element someone did, we can also retaliate and say spiteful subjects. You may not try this because you cannot stand for your self, however you may suppress your emotions. Our reactions often exacerbate situations and produce out the worst in us. The proper manner to cope with our emotions is to answer to them. This system includes deeply reflecting on the emotions after which making an informed choice. For example, for your case, your feelings of 'damage' on being ridiculed through a chum may be telling you approximately the way you want to step up for yourself and not allow each person to mistreat you.

• Once you have were given meditated on what that emotion manner, think about diverse procedures to reply to it, and pick all people choice you revel in addresses the state of affairs maximum as it should be. If you feel sad because of the reality your accomplice in no way prioritizes your choice and alternatively makes all of the important selections on my own, speak to your companion approximately it. Since you in no way oppose his/her thoughts or present your viewpoints, your partner may moreover count on that your consent on his/her alternatives is implied and is going collectively with what he/she feels is proper. Perhaps if you share your mind with him/her, it is able to assist him/her understand your sentiments.

Working on the ones areas on the equal time may be tough. As such, it's excellent to take subjects slow and consistent. There's no need to weigh down yourself thru searching for to do the whole lot immediately or looking to decorate your human beings-stunning dispositions in a single day.

You superior these behavioral inclinations over time; it'll take time to trade them too. Keep taking infant steps, and in case you live regular, you may conquer this problem.

As you begin accepting yourself and your feelings, you'll understand you have got got a preference. Please begin exercise this choice extra because exercising it can transform you from a susceptible character proper right into a sturdy character who's aware about what he/she desires and who can upward thrust up for that.

In the subsequent financial ruin, we'll discover this option extra so you can hold operating closer to being a more confident, self-confident character in location of a pushover and those pleaser:

Step #four: Realize You Have a Choice and Exercise it

Popular American writer John C. Maxwell as quickly as stated, "Life is an issue of options, and each choice you are making, makes you."

Since you are normally over-functioning, running spherical making sure your circle of relatives are satisfied and thrilled with you, you may believe you don't have each different preference.

You live silent when your brief-tempered companion yells at you because of the truth you experience your most effective desire is to keep queit. You supply your subjects to your traumatic pal because you observed you have not any different preference considering that refusing your buddy can also disillusioned him/her. Most of the stuff you do to pleasure others are often a end result of believing that there wasn't every different way out.

Sadly, that notion is wrong and restricting.

In every scenario you stumble upon, no matter how sincere or complicated it's miles, you constantly have a desire, on occasion you have got got a couple of choice!

You have a desire to mention no, the selection to set limitations, the choice to pick out phrases that don't allow human beings to mistreat you, and the choice to select and keep the proper human beings on your social circle.

This economic smash dreams to help you recognize and exercise those types of choices, and from it, come to be self-confident sufficient to stay a glad life for your terms.

The Choice to Say No

Yes, you constantly ALWAYS have the choice to say 'no' to everyone you don't feel comfortable obliging to. Think of techniques frivolously your colleague refuses to do your percent of difficult paintings if you ever request make the form of request, but how tough it's miles as a manner to do the identical. If others can say 'no' to you whenever they want, you could say no too whilst announcing sure doesn't fit your needs.

Refusing to run errands for people or skip above and past to assist a person does no longer propose you're impolite. It in reality technique that now and again you cannot and need to not over-characteristic; announcing no is virtually spotting this and then exercising your right to attain this.

Now that you recognize your emotions from being treated cruelly and unjustly by using manner of others, you'll be higher privy to the times you don't desire to oblige people and can't bypass overboard with a few component for them.

If a person asks you for a desire, desires you to run an errand for them, or requires some help you can't provide for any reason, say 'no.' Saying no might be difficult at the begin. However, even as you say no a couple of instances, refuse and stay sturdy, and artwork at the same traces once more, humans will sooner or later prevent bugging you.

You will rapid get the keep of saying 'no' at the same time as you don't have the time or electricity to run spherical for others and start enjoying more time at your disposal to do belongings you need.

Remember, whilst you refuse someone's request, keep away from giving vague and fake excuses.

For example:

If you can't work in your colleague's mission due to the reality you need to spend time collectively collectively with your own family, don't use the excuse of being unwell. Tell the person who you have got commitments at the facet of your circle of relatives, and because of the truth that your art work hours are over, you'd alternatively spend time with them. Give your answer, walk away, and don't appearance lower returned.

If you're saying no over a call or a message, be as easy and unique as feasible, and don't respond. It is ok; you could do this; in any case, we're speaking about your properly-being, that is paramount.

The Choice to Use Different Words

While you ought to say 'no' on every occasion needed and experience find it irresistible, first-class conditions may be difficult.

Besides 'yes' and 'no,' you've got were given many specific terms to pick from to in a well mannered way convey your message of now not following someone's directive in pick of doing a little thing you need.

Whenever a person asks you to do some element you but don't want to do, strive the subsequent hacks to deal with the scenario lightly and strongly:

- Don't rush to mention 'certain' or 'no' immediately. At such times, anxiety is likely to easy over you.

- Instead, pause and breathe deeply. Inhale thru your nostril, and exhale thru your mouth more than one instances to calm your annoying nerves. If taking breaths is difficult in front of someone, live placed and pause for some moments in advance than giving your answer.

- Based at the state of affairs you're in, think about a solution splendid than a 'no.' For example, if a colleague who's also a chum invitations you to a celebration, but you don't feel like going, you may say, 'I can try, but I'll in all likelihood be overdue; it's better if you circulate by myself. That way, I received't wreck your amusing.' If your lengthy-distance companion needs to have a video call with you each day, but that upsets your artwork recurring, advocate doing it every days because it will offer you with more subjects to speak about and percentage. If a salesclerk indicates you try some component, ask him for his massive variety so you can accumulate out to him later.

- Instead of outrightly rejecting someone, strive the usage of specific responses in extraordinary conditions to growth answers that satisfy each you and that exceptional person in that state of affairs.

Once you begin doing that, you'll recognise which you commonly have a desire to provide you new answers in place of giving in to every one-of-a-kind individual's whims or refusing them outright.

The Choice of Saying "I Don't" Instead of "I Can't."

When a humans pleaser begins offevolved announcing no to humans, such a person is possibly to mention, 'I can't do that.' You're probable to make the equal mistake. The trouble with saying 'I can't' is that it invites the opportunity character to say, 'Why even though?' which then pushes your obstacles.

You are possibly to inform insistent people that you can't attend the birthday celebration, can't do a wonderful assignment, or can't pick out their laundry. The instantaneous you try this, they ask why or provide you with massive reasons that in a few manner compels you to oblige to their requests.

The repair to this trouble is straightforward: bear in mind that proper here too, you have a desire: the selection of saying, 'I don't' in area of 'I can't.'

If you don't want to do some aspect, say, "I don't need to choose out your laundry" or "I don't want to paintings on your venture because of the reality I'm busy" and walk. Saying "I don't need to" is an assertive solution that suggests your loss of interest in walking for the other individual, this is possibly to shoo them away.

A have a look at posted within the Journal of Consumer Research in 2012 decided that the use of 'I don't' in preference to 'I can't' in everyday speech helped people gracefully stroll out of undesirable commitments.

'I don't is a effective response than 'I can't.' It rapid shuts down faux friends and poisonous human beings. It furthermore enables set up your obstacles and enables you come back off as a confident individual who's aware about a manner to prioritize his/her obligations and nicely-being. Try this hack each time you want to excuse your self from being a person's valet with dignity.

The Choice to Set Boundaries

Unfortunately, not plenty folks examine the significance and paintings of setting obstacles from an early age. Some human beings don't realise what limitations are, leave on my own the way to set them. Many others, particularly those dealt with as pushovers, conflict to famend the importance of putting obstacles once they were brutally crushed and disrespected.

Every dating is predicated upon at the values of understand, care, and reputation, all of which can't occur inside the absence of obstacles. Setting limitations refers to detailing how exclusive people can behave with you. Different relationships have first rate boundaries determined by way of the human beings concerned.

For instance, now not calling every one of a kind hurtful names is a healthful boundary in lots of relationships. If you don't like your accomplice checking your cellphone or invading your privateness or private area, that might be a few exclusive boundary you could set in that relationship.

Boundaries instill peace, clarity, recognize, popularity, and the records of giving every unique area in a relationship. So an extended manner, you haven't set many healthy boundaries in your relationships, it virtually is why humans find it clean to get their way with you.

You are invisible to them due to the fact you in no manner made them recognize that you exist. People ridicule you due to the fact you by no means stopped them from doing so. Nobody asks you about your options because of the truth you haven't made them recognize it became crucial to attain this.

Since you don't need human beings to hold mistreating you, here's how you could start setting healthy barriers in your relationships:

• Think of the manner the people you're in certainly one of a kind crucial relationships deal with you. Ensure you describe your emotions in detail and write them down to your mag.

• If you aren't satisfied with the remedy you're receiving, reflect onconsideration on how the opportunity way you want matters to be, making sure you supply an cause of that account in detail.

• Contrast the 2 conditions to apprehend why you've now not received the honour, care, and love you feel you deserve and the manner you could gain what you choice for—as defined inside the 2d account.

• Think of the bounds you need to set to bring about that alternate. For example, in case you don't need your companion to make crucial alternatives by myself, you need to talk that problem and located your foot down every time your associate makes an vital selection with out your enter or consent. If you don't respect your colleague using your mug, or starting up your table drawer to borrow a few stationery or pocket book, permit the colleague understand you don't appreciate that and would really like him/her to invite for permission in advance than the use of your topics. If you don't approve of your dad and mom taking money from your wallet without asking, in a polite manner deliver your message to them. Since you're an grownup now, they want to apprehend and recognize your limitations.

• Once you've got idea of the boundaries you want to set in brilliant relationships, talk those troubles with the relevant human beings. You need to clearly walk as a good deal as that individual, tell him/her you've got were given a few factor critical to percent, and specific your issues. You may inform the character you'd like to talk approximately a few factor with him/her, plan it, after which amicably percent your perspectives.

Remember to take it slow whilst talking, and don't permit the alternative person to interrupt you. In case that happens, firmly tell him/her to offer you your share of time to talk. If the occurrence repeats, get up and depart as it's continuously first-class to vacate a speak desk that doesn't serve appreciate.

- Once you have got communicated the bounds you'd need to set with the alternative human beings, start following them your self. For instance, in case you don't want a person to scream at you, make sure you communicate softly. Moreover, endure in thoughts to prevent over-functioning in every relationship because of the reality that's wherein you breach the boundary and inspire others to do the same.

As you begin setting wholesome, vast obstacles on your relationships, you can begin putting folks that mistreat you on a decent leash whilst developing a healthful scenario for loving relationships to bloom.

The Choice of Whom to Keep and Whom to Let Go Of

While you don't get to pick out your natural mother and father and siblings, you get to choose whom to be pals with, work with, socialize with, and construct relationships with.

Moreover, if you experience suffocated with and via even your organic circle of relatives members, don't neglect which you have a desire of parting strategies with them. As harsh because it sounds, every so often, parting techniques is the handiest manner to alleviate undue stress, pain, and trauma.

Not anybody around is loving and accepting sufficient to will assist you to be who you preference to be and acquire you with open arms. Also, no longer all and sundry respects and enables your thoughts and encourages you to pursue your objectives.

If you aren't too pleased with sure toxic human beings to your social circle, you constantly have the choice to allow skip of them.

What is 'toxic and what isn't always,' you may ask? Anything that makes you revel in suffocated, harm, rejected, and disrespected is poisonous. Anyone who sparks such emotions, ridicules you, insults your thoughts, maltreats you, and continues emotionally, verbally, and psychologically bullying you is poisonous.

All such impacts never help you live a satisfied, fulfilled life. Rather, they humiliate you and maintain you from growing into your unique and effective self. Determine all such affects on your life, and slowly distance your self from them.

With a few toxic humans, you can element methods right away. If that's the case, don't hesitate to accomplish that. You have already discovered to exercise your proper of saying 'no,' so skip in advance and permit the toxic humans to your existence understand how you don't want to have them round.

For toxic human beings that you can't cut ties with right away, slowly distance your self from them. Stop assembly toxic colleagues out of doors of labor, don't take calls from demanding friends who sabotage your self assurance, and block immodest buddies who misuse you and take benefit of your kindness.

As you detach yourself from the poisonous human beings in your existence, you create room for every person who genuinely love you. Reach out to such people, and spend extra time with them.

In case letting move of toxic humans doesn't go away you with many loving and supportive humans, find out extra of your type by using using the use of assembly extra humans, attending social gatherings, and searching up like-minded human beings in assist businesses or social media companies of your locality/area/metropolis.

If you start walking on these tips with determination, you'll word a marked improvement in how you believe you studied, enjoy, and behave. To keep the momentum growing, art work on boosting your self-self warranty. The subsequent bankruptcy guides you in element approximately that.

Chapter 5: Boost Your Self-Confidence

Australian golfer Jason Day says, "When you've got an entire lot of self warranty, and also you enjoy like no person can beat you, it's game over for each person else."

Confidence is the notion or feeling of relying on some element or someone. When you revel in assured in a person, you consider the man or woman's potential to do a little thing or judgment to make the right alternatives.

So an extended way, you have got got depended on people too much, even in phrases of personal alternatives. Whether you had to determine what get dressed/tuxedo to area on to your buddy's bridal ceremony, what path to look at, profession to choose out, or whether or not or not to honestly take delivery of a cutting-edge machine provide, you constantly appeared as a good deal as a person to make the final call.

Do you understand why? It because of the truth to this point, you've had more self belief in other human beings's judgment, intelligence, and talents than in yours.

When you over and over rely upon someone else's judgment and skills, you allow them to accept as actual with in how an awful lot you charge them. Sadly, many people will be inclined to abuse this appreciation. They revel in superior and then try to control and manipulate you turning you into their valet who is continuously taking walks their errands.

Since you have got got were given determined to expose over a contemporary day leaf, it's miles now time to construct yourself guarantee in preference to relying on a person else's. Self-self guarantee is vital on your physical and highbrow properly-being.

When you in reality keep in mind on your competencies, you price your self, devote your electricity and time to doing crucial duties, check with first-rate thoughts and sports sports in existence, make greater wholesome and happier way of life alternatives, and foster vast relationships.

If you've got been following the incredible pointers shared inside the previous chapters, you can have already determined a large self perception growth. Here is what you can maintain doing to growth this self perception with the useful resource of manifolds:

\#: Change your narrative

People pleasers discover a difficult time stunning others if they're now not performing some component special for them. Unless and till you are at your friend's consistent beck and communicate to, or assisting him/her in all their loopy antics, or giggling at their jokes, they obtained't be satisfied with you.

You also can moreover have attempted to have an effect on human beings by means of way of way of displaying off your intelligence or entertain them through using cracking funny jokes, which, maximum possibly, didn't forestall nicely for you. You revel in invisible round all of the folks who use you whilst you aren't doing them any want.

Moreover, due to the reality you often get keep of the bloodless shoulder, you are possibly to have many embarrassing moments on your credit score score at the same time as you felt terrible approximately your self. Naturally, this takes a toll in your self perception and self-perception. Things don't should be that manner.

According to a test posted inside the American Psychological Association, if you alter your narrative, you could trade the way you keep in mind you studied and experience, and therefore, growth yourself perception. The have a look at accumulated statistics from over 3 hundred humans, with their recollections divided into instructions.

The first institution of memories had redemption sequences in which properly effects accompanied terrible activities. The second set of stories had 'infection sequences' in which correct sports ended in unfortunate outcomes.

The effects showed that folks who knowledgeable more redemption tales were happier and extra confident than folks that advocated contamination testimonies. This studies shows how a satisfied finishing makes us glad and illustrates our strength over rewriting our recollections and converting our narrative for the higher.

That approach, regardless of how terrible your scenario or tale is, in case you rewrote it and knowledgeable it in order that the very last results feels first rate, you could revel in higher and consequently improve your self perception.

To exercise this method, do the subsequent:

• Think of the maximum flinch-truly really worth or embarrassing 2nd you can't neglect. If you've got were given too a number of those, write they all down in descending order, transferring from the maximum awkward tale to the least embarrassing one.

• Recall that enjoy in your head, and think about the way you felt at that point.

• Think of methods the people round you behaved at that thing. Did they haughtily snigger at you, jeer, or ridicule you? Did every person display any issue or assist?

• Next, shift the focus from your self to those spherical you. Think of the factors of interest, sounds, activities connected to that situation. If someone else behaved in a stupid way, hold in mind that. If you have got been sitting in a brightly lit room even as that uncomfortable episode befell, don't forget that.

• Now consider what you located from the revel in. Did the incidence advantage you in any manner? Did you provide price to a person? How has that enjoy modified you for the better? Think of all the ones matters, and write them down.

• Play the entire episode in your mind once more, however this time, do it the usage of the unique commands you sincerely observed out. When you be conscious it beneath a one-of-a-kind moderate, you apprehend it in any other case. The identical story that in advance appeared disconcerting and appalling to you currently does no longer appear that awful. It is probably to appear fun, specific, extremely good, or something from which you may research a treasured lesson about your self or those spherical you.

It may be super to have interaction in this exercising as quickly as every day at the same time as you remember any awkward 2nd you've got been thru and improve your narrative. By doing this, slowly, you may learn how to rewrite your every day stories certainly and examine from them. Naturally, even as you recognize special situations clearly, you experience more self-confident and can be your authentic self within the the front of others.

#: Improve your frame language

Harvard Professor Amy Cuddy's research on body language suggests that we typically have t frame language kinds: excessive and coffee strength frame language.

High energy body language includes postures in that you preserve your head high, all over again instantly, maintain direct eye touch with others, and hold your limbs open. Low energy body language entails retaining your head low, once more slouched, limbs closed, and you refrain from searching someone in the eye.

Her studies additionally showed that high power frame language boosts your testosterone ranges, whilst low electricity frame language lowers the ones tiers. Testosterone is a hormone related to self guarantee and exuberance, because of this that whilst its degrees are immoderate, you sense more poised and strong, and when they lower, you revel in the opportunity.

As a human beings pleaser and someone who not often gets a good buy attention, you experience beneath-assured, this is probably to translate into low electricity frame language. Like you found out to shape yourself guarantee thru changing your narrative, you may take it up a notch with the resource of enhancing your frame language.

Here's how you may do that:

- Stand right away together together with your ft at hip-distance aside. Keep your again proper now, keep your head a bit immoderate, tilt your chin upward, and appearance immediately. Maintain this pose for two mins and hold taking deep breaths. Also referred to as the 'Superman/Wonder Woman' pose, this pose improves your posture and self perception.

- Whether you're walking, sitting, or reputation straight away, make certain to carry out that via maintaining your lower back right away, head held forwards, and shoulders extraordinary and open.

- Keep your legs without delay and open, and your palms by way of the use of your aspects or at the table when fame/sitting.

- Always maintain direct eye contact at the same time as speaking to come backtrack as an assertive man or woman who is privy to what he/she is pronouncing.

- Moreover, smile at the same time as greeting people or attractive with them because it portrays you as an amicable and assured individual.

The following image in reality distinguishes among excessive and espresso strength body poses; undertake the previous and chorus from the latter.

As you beautify your body language, you'll experience more confident and find it smooth to behave strongly in challenging conditions.

#: Love yourself

Self-love is magical, and its energy is unequalled. When you love yourself, you bathe time and hobby onto your self, nourishing your mind and soul, making you sense alive. Like actress Lucille Ball says, "Love your self first and the whole thing else falls into line. You sincerely have to love your self to get some thing finished on this international."

You have usually looked for love and admiration from the ones round you, and at the same time as you don't acquire it, you experience miserable, which cripples yourself guarantee.

Here are some changes you can make in your existence to begin loving yourself to sense stronger and extra self-confident.

• Spend splendid time with yourself each day and use that factor to do some issue that relaxes, energizes, excites, or soothes you. You should take a look at your chosen ebook, watch a film, move for a stroll, exercising, order takeout and enjoy it by myself, or do some thing that comforts you. You also can have one-of-a-type activities for notable days, thereby developing rituals of sorts. For example, Mondays can be portray days, Tuesdays for biking, Wednesday for yoga, and so forth.

• Start pursuing sports that convey you meaning and rate. If you don't like membership-hopping together collectively together with your friends, forestall doing that. Instead, take that Zumba elegance you've generally desired to take.

• Prioritize your vital responsibilities and goals, and find time for them. If your once more hurts, but you've been averting travelling the chiropractor because of the fact your commitments to awesome human beings absorb all your time, usually have a propensity for your need now. Ensure you create a every day agenda wherein your vital duties and goals are your precedence.

• Stop comparing your self and your lifestyles to that of others. Seeing a friend pressure a Mercedes may additionally furthermore go away you yearning for one, specially if you don't very own a vehicle. However, inside the course of such times, don't spiral into negativity; rely variety your benefits. Go thru all of your benefits and nurture gratitude. Accept that everybody is going through a private conflict that they may no longer show, and also you need to be happy with what you have got were given.

• Spend time with loving humans being your real self so that you can begin feeling extra snug for your pores and pores and skin and unharness your proper self.

You have untapped capability interior you. All you want to do is recognize this, tap into that energy, and allow it shine your way.

You can do this masses, and you're nicely worth loving! Just examine the steerage on this ebook, and shortly, you'll launch your quality existence to date.

Chapter 6: Please Stop Pleasing

There is a distinction among a peacemaker and a people-pleaser. A peacemaker desires to achieve a choice and restore stability. They try and see the issue from all sides objectively and rationally. A peacemaker wants to help others, notwithstanding the fact that it manner telling the fact, which might also furthermore harm. They inform it like it's far, even though the human beings concerned don't want to face truth.

On the opposite hand, a human beings-pleaser dreams anybody spherical them to be satisfied, so they may essentially perform a little component every person asks of them. Saying effective to humans may be a dependancy for a few humans-pleasers, at the same time as for others, it has turn out to be an addiction that makes them enjoy as even though they're wished. Constantly saying certain to others makes the humans-pleaser revel in useful and vital—like they're which consist of rate to a person else's existence.

Being a human beings-pleaser furthermore comes from the want to create an interpersonal bridge to others. This bridge is our connection with unique people via diverse kinds of bonds or shared critiques. Typically, this bridge is created thru own family relationships, college, artwork sports activities, being neighborly, common interests, sharing comparable values, or having relatable life evaluations.

HIGHLY SENSITIVE PEOPLE AND PEOPLE-PLEASING

Being a reasonably sensitive individual makes being a human beings-pleaser even extra complicated. In popular, our relationships are extra difficult due to the truth our values vary notably from the ones around us. When it involves relationships, we may moreover moreover even experience deprived due to the fact we aren't aggressive and are trying to find mutuality, no longer a opposition. As HSPs, we often fail to get the honor we deserve because of the fact our empathy and kindness are not valued. HSPs feel like they don't belong with exclusive humans. We enjoy the arena so in a fantastic way and can fail to amplify interpersonal bridges. This leaves us feeling lonely and misunderstood, which ends up in us turning to humans-appealing to get the social reputation we are craving.

Our want to people-please surfaces whilst seeking out to in shape in with a group, like a work surroundings or circle of relatives. We need to gain some social standing, however they may be precise from us. In any situation, people-charming comes from wondering that the responsibility to build the interpersonal bridge is ours. Unless we established plenty extra strive, a connection might not form.

HSPs are also probably to be people-pleasers due to the truth we dislike warfare. We are involved that if we are saying no to someone or talk our thoughts, we'll cause the opposite individual to feel disenchanted or harm. Before we even get a chance to say no, our minds run away with us, growing situations of the uncomfortable conditions that might get up. HSPs observe exceptional people with out difficulty, so we choose out up on diffused displeasure or anger (or possibly we accept as true with the opportunity character is unhappy). This reasons us to revel in responsible or ashamed, and we turn out to be saying fantastic. We additionally discover it hard to simply take delivery of grievance, and those-fascinating is a way to keep away from being criticized.

When we experience the need to humans-please, we are doing more than crucial in our relationships. People-captivating locations us in a function in which we enjoy now not so correct as the opposite character in some way. It is how we cover our "one of a kindness" and a way for us to live to inform the tale in a social environment in which we enjoy deprived.

Causes of human beings-appealing

Various factors can also moreover moreover play a position in people-appealing:

1. Poor vanity. People are regularly people-pleasers due to the fact they don't rate their very personal goals and dreams. A loss of self-self belief reasons a need for outside validation, and those-pleasers experience that saying certain to others and doing favors will motive popularity and approval.

2. Insecurity. In other times, humans can also emerge as people-pleasers because they're worried that human beings acquired't like or take delivery of them within the event that they don't cross above and past to make others glad.

three. Perfectionism. Some human beings want the whole thing to be "actually right' which incorporates how precise humans assume and enjoy.

four. Past studies. Traumatic, difficult, or painful opinions also can play a detail in humans-lovely. People who've suffered thru abuse or rejection also can try and please others to keep away from conflict or revel in abandoned. They will attempt the entirety possible to make different human beings satisfied to avoid triggering abusive behavior.

Effects of being a humans-pleaser

Being a human beings-pleaser isn't continuously a terrible element. Being a being involved and worried man or woman is an important a part of preserving a healthy dating. However, it will become a problem even as you're seeking to win approval or are pursuing happiness on the rate of your private emotional and highbrow nicely-being.

The following are some of the consequences of being a human beings-pleaser:

1. Anger and Frustration. While you could experience helping others, you also are fine to experience a few anger or frustration while you're doing things out of responsibility or reluctance. These terrible emotions can cause a cycle of helping someone, feeling anger or frustration in the direction of them for taking benefit, after which feeling regretful or sorry for yourself.

2. Anxiety and Stress. Constantly keeping others glad can stretch your private mental, emotional, and bodily assets too thin. Trying to manipulate how humans experience can depart you with now not something but pressure and anxiety, that would detrimentally have an effect on your fitness.

3. Depleted Willpower. With all your electricity and intellectual assets spent on making sure unique people are glad, you have got were given a great deal much less electricity of will to address your own dreams and care for your very very very own wishes. Willpower and strength of will can be restricted assets, normal with contemporary studies.1 Spending all your strength of will on others leaves you with little left to decide to yourself.

4. Lack of Authenticity. People-pleasers regularly disguise their non-public needs, opinions, or possibilities to residence others. This will make you sense like you're no longer residing an proper lifestyles, nearly like you don't honestly apprehend who you're.

five. Weaker Relationships. The people for your life might also understand your giving nature, however subsequently, they'll moreover begin to take your kindness and willingness to assist as a right. People may not even recognise they're taking advantage of you. They just recognize you're constantly inclined to help, just so they do no longer doubt that you'll be there every time help is desired. What they will not see is how overcommitted and thinly stretched you may be. Putting in all of your efforts to fulfill special human beings's expectancies might also leave you feeling envious.

HOW PEOPLE-PLEASING AFFECTS YOUR RELATIONSHIPS

Throughout my early life, most of my relationships were one-sided; I, the giver of my time, and others glad to get preserve of my generosity. I in no way confused this imbalance due to the truth, in my mind, it turned into simply the manner the vicinity labored. I continually said sure and modified into constantly exhausted, overwhelmed, overcommitted, and depressing.

One day I found a habitual problem remember in my lifestyles–resentment. In trendy, the feeling that observed my loss of ability to say no changed into resentment. My overgiving added about me feeling inexperienced with envy in the direction of the people in my life.

People-appealing in relationships may look like an tremendous element. After all, whilst you're with a person, helping them and making them glad is essential. As a people-pleaser, you're doing each, right? Maybe. However, you're likely often doing it at your private price. By human beings-lovely, you may not quality lose touch collectively in conjunction with your private options and desires however even have a buildup of silent resentment. Instead of voicing your emotions, you switch out to be keeping immediately to anger that your companion isn't even privy to, all due to the reality you're in search of to keep away from struggle.

Over time, the resentment and sadness might also want to reason you seeking a connection a few area else or leaving the connection. All even as your accomplice wasn't even conscious there was a hassle.

Here are a number of the approaches people-captivating can be hurting your relationships:

1. If we are the ones doing the whole lot for our own family contributors, friends, and co-personnel, they are no longer going to experience boom. By continuously being to be had to assist, we restrict their capability to tackle new responsibilities. When we're now not spherical, they may not entire the responsibilities successfully due to the reality they will no longer recognise what to do on their private.

2. Our people-charming behavior deny other human beings the opportunity to assist us and love us equitably. If the humans on your life don't understand your goals, they're able to't satisfy them.

3. By continuously people-attractive, our movements create indebtedness. This isn't some issue that is verbally agreed upon however makes others feel like they're held hostage and want to repay us for our sacrifice.

4. People-charming relationships are frequently primarily based mostly on dishonesty (or, at least, not whole disclosure). This manner the relationship we've were given with others isn't continuously actual. If we can not be sincere about what we want in a relationship, deliver our opinion all through a communique, or talk what sincerely brings us pleasure, our accomplice gained't recognize who we sincerely are. It moreover makes it tough for anybody to recognize the way to love us. When our communications are most effective partial truths or our interactions are dishonest or incomplete, it degrades the keep in mind and connection a number of the alternative man or woman and us. Our relationships also can lack authenticity.

WHY PEOPLE-PLEASING IS SO DANGEROUS FOR HSPS

People-attractive regularly has the alternative impact than what is meant. We, as humans-pleasers, may also try to get a notable response from others, however as a substitute, we make human beings experience subtly uneasy. So why is being extraordinary attentive and self-sacrificing met with awkwardness and avoidance? Why does this result in people feeling uneasy in choice to thankful? Well, it activates a "spider-sense" in maximum people and leaves others subconsciously wondering, "Why is this man or woman so concerned with how I experience? Why are they so eager to pride? Are they hiding a few component?"

Someone with none seen dreams or goals doesn't appear proper. It is likewise no longer possible not to have want and desires. This is why human beings also can experience uneasy around us. When we cross proper right into a human beings-fascinating mode, which is basically to cover our proper selves, specific humans also can experience wary around us. Often, they don't even understand why. This outcomes in them subtly retreating from us, and due to our heightened perception, this rejection can be painful.

Unfortunately, maximum tremendously sensitive people respond to rejection and social awkwardness thru humans-ideal even more. This results in a vicious cycle of people-appealing observed with the aid of exhaustion, defeat, and excessive feelings of rejection. It becomes truly overwhelming—but it is so hard to save you ideal everybody.

WHY IS IT DIFFICULT TO STOP PEOPLE-PLEASING?

The quick solution is that humans-stunning is a safety mechanism. It is a technique for protection. It is a way for people to comply even as confronted with a tough or uncomfortable situation.

At the middle, people-pleasers are fearful of rejection. Everyone fears rejection, however rejection is worse for HSPs. Often people-appealing is installed to trauma. In a few times, a humans-pleaser may have experienced rejection from their caregivers on enough sports to doubt the constancy of diverse human beings's love. They feel like they want to perform or earn love with the aid of behaving in beneficial or captivating procedures. In practice, this rejection need to look like a breakup or a fallout amongst near buddies. It is probably some component greater subtle, like getting the silent remedy from a member of the family for days or possibly weeks at a time. People-pleasers often extend up in families wherein affection and love are based totally on traditional ordinary overall performance. This isn't best instructional or athletic performance; it may be appearing thru doing what they're knowledgeable. For example, in a single household, the unspoken rule might be to expose little or no emotion. This type of "pull your self collectively" mentality is a shape of rejection. So the unstated rule in this family can be some thing like: "Don't speak approximately what you're feeling, and we'll get alongside truly wonderful." Anyone who breaks this rule receives branded as a drama queen, too emotional, too sensitive, or an excessive amount of. All of those labels are a shape of rejection and judgment.

Most human beings-pleasers I understand were categorized as 'too much.' The unhappy paradox of this case is that quite touchy human beings's "undesired or ugly" emotions might be heightened in a circle of relatives just like the above example. This just brings about a cycle of rejection and struggle. The man or woman's feelings can be soothed whilst they're compassionately acknowledged, and that usually comes from performing some component that makes someone glad, aka people-fascinating.

In every different circle of relatives, the unstated rule can also need to do with success and excellence. If the kid is on the pinnacle of their beauty or plays nicely, they acquire love. A little one in this own family develops overall performance-based arrogance. Essentially, all of their emotions of self confidence come from what they do in preference to who they will be. While this individual may be a shining movie star, they don't have a revel in of their very very own intrinsic self confidence. They test that taking dangers is a no-skip, and their creativity and voice are regularly stifled with the aid of using fear of failure and in the long run being rejected for failing.

A individual from a circle of relatives like this has in no way had the essential protection to find out their non-public selections or creativity. They have been usually too busy looking for to take the temperature of the room. They constantly had to determine out what others have been feeling and in want of to assume and deal with those desires. This is regularly referred to as parentification by using therapists. This is whilst a infant or youngster takes at the region of soothing, nurturing, or tending to their parents or unique adults in hopes they may obtain praise.

Children who develop as much as be human beings-pleasers live with a danger setting over them—the hazard of rejection. The risk of "otherwise": "Do this in any other case I won't love you anymore." And if the child does the other of what is predicted, they revel in rejection.

Another motive humans find it tough to break the humans-attractive cycle is due to the truth when they perform a touch thing that makes others happy, they acquire splendid reinforcement. This does a incredible manner of boosting their self guarantee and standard overall performance-primarily based absolutely arrogance (as a minimum for a touch at the equal time as). Other human beings get to gain from all their generosity, and that they get a self warranty increase. However, the admiration is brief-lived, and as quickly because it wears off, they enjoy the need to people-please once more.

Often, humans discover it difficult to save you humans-appealing because of the reality there may be no easy opportunity. Even if someone is capable of art work thru their worry of war and rejection, the crippling guilt that includes putting barriers and many precise hallmark functions of this conduct is difficult to overcome. People-pleasers frequently default to being caregivers and fascinating others due to the fact they haven't had the protection or region to determine out an possibility manner of being within the global. Breaking free from being a people-pleaser takes try to a multifaceted method. Numerous components want to be addressed to in fact take your electricity once more. The proper news is that it's far all absolutely possible!

BREAKING FREE FROM PEOPLE-PLEASING

People-acceptable is a behavior that may be tough to triumph over. Fortunately, there are some steps you could take to forestall being a people-pleaser. You can discover ways to stability your preference to make others glad with out sacrificing your private desires.

1. Establish boundaries.

It is vital to recognize your limits, establish smooth limitations, and then be willing to speak those limits and barriers. Be precise and clean about what you are inclined to tackle. If it seems like a person is soliciting for an excessive amount of from you, allow them to realize it's miles over the boundaries of what you're inclined to do, and also you received't be able to help them. There also are some precise techniques to create obstacles in your existence to help overcome your human beings-charming dispositions. For example, putting limitations on even as you're in a function to talk and most effective answering your cellphone inside the route of tremendous times.

2. Start small.

Changing a behavioral sample can be hard. It can be tough to make a shocking exchange for your humans-appealing conduct, so it's far often simpler to begin preserving yourself in small procedures. In many scenarios, you need to learn how to restrain yourself similarly to artwork on schooling the humans spherical you to recognize your limits. This is lots to do multi feature pass, so it is able to be beneficial to begin with a few small steps that help you parent in the direction of being much less of a human beings-pleaser. Begin with the aid of way of announcing no to smaller requests, ask for a few element you need, or strive expressing your opinion approximately some component small. For example, start thru pronouncing no to a request via text. Then art work your way as a bargain as saying no in character. Practice this in brilliant conditions or settings, like even as ordering at a restaurant, speakme to a salesclerk, or coping with a co-worker. It moreover helps to start putting obstacles with those who are much more likely to comprehend them. Create excellent stories by using way of beginning with smaller, tons less complex ones which will educate your anxious machine and thoughts that that is a strong and wholesome workout.

3. Set desires and priorities.

Think about wherein you want to spend it gradual and electricity. What dreams are you aiming to carry out? Who do you want to assist? When you recognize your priorities, you may be able to determine if you have the time and strength to commit to some component. If you discover that some issue or a person is draining your power or the usage of too much of a while, take the essential steps to deal with the problem. When you begin putting your barriers into workout and announcing no to the assets you don't want to do, you will find out you have got greater time and electricity to decide to the vital matters on your existence.

4. Stall for time.

When a person asks you for a prefer, inform them you want time to don't forget it. You can respond with, "Let me get again to you on that" or "I don't have my calendar on me; permit me test once I get a minute." Saying fine right away might also moreover leave you feeling obligated and overcommitted. However, taking the time to reply to someone's request will provide you with the time you want to anticipate it through and decide if it's some issue you would love to tackle. Before you're making the choice, ask your self:

- How burdened will I be if I say sure?
- How a good buy time is that this going to take?
- Do I actually have the time to do it?
- Is it some detail I really need to do?
- Will this be uplifting or draining?

Research has moreover demonstrated that even a quick pause (and a deep breath) in advance than finding out will boom choice-making accuracy. When you offer your self a 2d, it is going to be much less complicated in case you need to because it have to be determine if it's a venture you've got got time for and want to take on.

five. Assess the request.

Another step you may take inside the direction of overcoming your human beings-proper trait is to search for any signal that someone may be seeking to take benefit of your generosity. Is the request coming from a person who generally seems to want some issue from you however is unavailable at the same time as you need them to go back the selection? Are a few people aware of your beneficiant nature and ask because of the fact they understand you received't say no? If you experience like you're being manipulated into performing some thing, take the time to assess what you're being asked to do and determine the way you need to address the request. If someone maintains taking gain of your kindness and insisting you have to assist, be organisation and easy approximately your selection no longer to assist.

6. Avoid making excuses.

It is important to be direct when you say no and don't blame exclusive responsibilities or make excuses in your disability to assist or take at the assignment. When you start explaining why you could't do a little element, you offer certainly one of a kind people the threat to poke holes via your excuse. Explaining your cause in the back of pronouncing no additionally gives them the chance to change their request to make certain you can despite the fact that do what they're asking. Try and use a decisive tone whilst you assert no to a few factor and withstand the urge to characteristic vain element about your reasoning. Remember, "No" is an entire sentence.

7. Relationships require provide and take.

A strong and healthy courting consists of a wonderful diploma of mutuality. If one individual is continuously giving and the possibility is continuously taking, it regularly method one in every of them is forgoing their needs to ensure the opportunity individual has what they want. Even if you enjoy making exclusive people glad, it's far critical to bear in mind that they should furthermore be giving to you in cross again.

eight. Create a mantra.

Create an empowering mantra and stick it someplace you can see it regularly, like to your mirror, as a records for your mobile phone, or next on your computer. This mantra will act as a mini pep talk at some point of the day. Here are some to attempt:

- I am allowed to mention no
- A no to them is a sure to me
- "No" is an entire sentence
- Not my circus, now not my monkeys (continuously makes me snigger)
- I don't owe everybody a proof
- I am the parent of my time and strength

nine. Say no with conviction.

As a human beings-pleaser, you may be tempted to mention "maybe" or "I don't understand" to an invite, regardless of the truth that you're not involved. Instead, use an effective and polite way to say no. If saying the phrase "no" outright appears a bit harsh, attempt this form of:

- Unfortunately, I'm at complete capability.

- I received't be capable of make it.

- I'll want to bypass on that challenge.

- I really have plans that day but thanks for taking into account me.

- I am honored, however a person else is probably extra suitable to devote the time that merits.

10. Sit with the pain.

For maximum people, specially HSPs, human beings-alluring is a manner to relieve the acute feelings of pain as regards to rejection, feeling less-than-ideal, or abandonment. However, in case you discover ways to sit down with those uncomfortable emotions and breathe via them, they'll have much less strength over your moves.

11. Help at the equal time as you want to assist.

Overcoming your human beings-stunning inclinations doesn't suggest you want to give up being considerate and sort. These are all suitable traits that make contributions to more potent, lasting relationships. However, you need to test your motivations and intentions. Don't handiest do topics because you worry rejection or searching for the approval of others. Continue doing proper matters but do them to your private phrases. Being a type character doesn't name for interest or rewards. It genuinely calls for the choice to make matters higher for someone else however no longer on the price of your happiness.

12. Examine why you enjoy forced to pride with the aid of journaling on the ones turns on.

The following questions will help you recognize the root purpose of your people-appealing: (this may be mainly eye-starting off, take preserve of a pen and paper and free write for at the least 3 mins in line with query; it's miles going to be well worth it!)

• Which relationships make me sense the need to please human beings?

- How do I depend on one-of-a-kind humans for resources of any kind that motive me to be in a humans-proper courting?

- What modifications do I want to make to reduce my dependency on others to have fewer relationships in which I want to pleasure?

- If I can't lessen my desires, what are the possibility answers that guide my self-recognize?

- Am I capable of create what I want?

- Am I capable of ask for more of what I need from my one-sided relationships to create more mutuality?

thirteen. Understand you could't control everything.

Let unique people make their private choices and feature their very own reactions. It allows to sincerely take delivery of which you can not control particular people's emotions. No rely what you do, someone is going to disapprove. You can't win all and sundry over. It is better to allow specific human beings be and take shipping of how they feel, even though it's a terrible emotion within the direction of you. At the prevent of the day, the handiest opinion approximately yourself that topics is yours.

14. Celebrate your development.

Overcoming people-lovable is tough work, and hundreds of people aren't inclined to place inside the attempt and get uncomfortable. Take the time to have a awesome time your achievements, irrespective of how small. Keep a self belief document, if you want to be a list for your cellular phone, of all of the methods you're analyzing to prevent human beings-attractive. Each time you want a self perception growth, discuss with it.

15. Seek professional guide.

There isn't always any shame in seeking out the assist of a expert. Trauma remedy plans like Eye Movement Desensitization and Reprocessing (EMDR), hypnotherapy, psychotherapy and counseling will let you technique any stressful reminiscences that have added on the need for humans-captivating. Therapy can assist get rid of any fear, anxiety, and guilt that includes inquiring for help, soliciting for your desires to be met, or saying no to someone.

Chapter 7: No Is Your Biggest Weapon

As we discussed in Chapter three, HSPs experience the want to be of enterprise. We are people-pleasers. We have a hard time announcing no to others. We find out it hard to mention no due to the truth we dislike war of words. We find out it less complicated to mention certain to everybody and make them glad because which means there's a slim chance of any struggle breaking out. Always pronouncing positive to human beings makes us experience like we're supportive and useful. For a short term, their acknowledgment of our moves makes us experience satisfied and wanted. The trouble that carries now not having the functionality to mention no is that we grow to be wishing different people may additionally reciprocate our movements, and we bottle up resentment closer to them.

SAYING NO AS AN HSP

One of the toughest commands I've needed to analyze in my existence and career is the importance of announcing no. The phrase no is not one that ever got here simply to me, as I suspect with many unique HSPs. I end up always eager to be a group participant and lend a assisting hand. It wasn't until I began out to say no to obligations, possibilities, and people that were no longer consistent with my center values and imaginative and prescient that I made significant strides in my life. Our capability to say no is a valuable information. Without it, it's almost now not viable to acquire our visions and goals.

So why is it so difficult to say no as an HSP? There are numerous complicating elements. The biggest contributor to our conflict with pronouncing no is due to the truth we feel everything very strongly. We additionally take in the emotions of those spherical us and sense them as even though they had been our own. Our empathy and sensitivity select up on the opportunity character's feelings, and we can tell within the event that they need us to say certain. The disappointment we don't forget the alternative person will revel in if we are saying no "guilts" us into announcing fantastic due to the reality we don't need to upset high-quality humans. Because we're so sensitive even as someone says no to us, it hurts extra, and we take it for my part. We moreover relate to humans emotionally, so due to the fact we understand how a tremendous deal being informed no can harm, we don't need to inflict that ache on others (in spite of the truth that a non-HSP likely wouldn't be too).

We are terrified of rejection and war. If we are saying no to others, we risk scary them, which in our minds will purpose battle. If we don't make them satisfied, we run the risk of them rejecting us. In the mind of an HSP, it is a lure-twenty- state of affairs. Saying sure to others in preference to placing our goals first leaves plenty less room for abandonment than saying no does.

HSPs are often informed we are blessed due to our objects and want to provide lower back. We're made to sense like we owe the arena due to the truth we were born with blessings manner to our sensitivity. This feeling of owing each person our time and expertise doesn't help with announcing no. We nearly sense accountable due to the truth then we're denying people our enterprise.

The people spherical us furthermore consciously or unconsciously pick up on the truth that we're touchy and inclined to help. Often, they will take benefit, specially if you're in the health or hospitality agency. Family and pals may also additionally anticipate unfastened remedies and count on you'll provide it to them because of your beneficiant nature. Clients can also name out of administrative center time in a catastrophe. Our inner want to selflessly assist others method we are probable to offer in to the ones humans.

Not saying no may also be ingrained in some HSPs in the occasion that they grew up in dysfunctional families. Saying no might have been volatile within the case of an abusive determine. You can also have had an excessive amount of duty located in your shoulders at a more youthful age, and also you couldn't say no to looking after your siblings. Growing up with a adolescence like that reasons someone to trust that the simplest secure and logical answer is positive because of the reality that's all they've ever identified. It feels remote places to say no. Saying sure will become a technique for coping.

THE IMPORTANCE OF SAYING NO

Learning to say no is vital for loads motives. Constantly announcing sure to others will drain our strength emotionally, mentally, and bodily. When we examine to mention no while it's important, we regain the power we need to cope with the important troubles in our lives. Saying no approach pronouncing sure to ourselves. We might be able to hold our very own health intact simply so we are able to shine our mild more efficiently. We can be rejuvenated and complete of electricity so that once we choose out to say high quality, we will assist others efficaciously. Saying no to any conditions or humans that don't in reality serve us will permit us the time we want to heal from any beyond trauma. This will assist us become greater balanced and related—bodily, mentally, energetically, and spiritually.

We can't truely take care of others if we're now not taking care of ourselves, and we're able to't address ourselves if we're commonly worn-out from saying positive to others. Saying no may be specifically tough in case you are the sort of man or woman who is usually making sure all people else is okay. Your giving and worrying nature is a super gift to offer the humans for your existence. However, to make sure you may hold offering that loving care, you want to ensure your desires are met first. Saying no is an important trouble for self-care. Setting healthy limitations will help us have the emotional and bodily reserve we want to help others without dropping ourselves in the approach.

Saying no is imperative due to the fact we permit special people preserve themselves and are available to their private conclusions in choice to us jumping to the rescue each time. If we're continuously assisting other humans, they'll forget about approximately that they're capable as properly. They will sincerely rely on us while it might be greater healthful for them to learn how to locate their very private manner. Making errors is probably what they want of their lifestyles to investigate and amplify.

Saying no is also essential due to the fact it's miles a signal of admire, as bizarre as that sounds. Saying sure to a person whilst we simply don't need to may additionally moreover reason resentment, negatively impacting our relationship with them. Saying no while that's what we advise indicates respect for ourselves and the opportunity character because of the truth we're real and honest, which may be characteristics that cultivate a healthy relationship. Another important motive to mention no is as it models this conduct for others in our lives. It gadgets a pleasing example of the importance of saying no. By pronouncing no, we'd inspire the human beings in our lives to set their non-public wholesome barriers with us and others within the destiny.

Saying no to as a minimum one component approach simultaneously announcing positive to a few component else. Respectfully declining an occasion or some thing that would have taken up our time technique we in reality said sure to the usage of that point for some factor we'd determine upon. This ought to suggest extra sleep, going to a yoga class, an middle of the night of movies, or extra time with our cherished ones.

Saying no manner we get to take breaks from converting the world. We get to gather wholesome boundaries. We get to loosen up and take that tour we've been dreaming of. We get to say no and be an HSP.

HOW TO SAY NO AS AN HSP

All of the HSP tendencies could make it revel in impossible to say no. However, with a hint little bit of boundary placing and some exercising, you will be properly in your manner to pronouncing sure to yourself.

Here are some extraordinary methods to build up self assure and authority within the again of that no:

1. Find the extent of socialization that feels proper for you.

Find a stability that works for you in which you're no longer continuously at the skip so much which you exhaust your self and are not bored from constantly looking for to avoid overstimulating conditions. Finding the proper degree of socialization will make announcing no less hard. You might be surrounded with the aid of close buddies who recognize your nature and gained't get angry whilst you need a day journey. By being in stability, you received't experience so worn-out and could have time for self-care and self-improvement.

2. Identify what's critical to you and make the selection to guard that point.

Take the time to parent out what makes you glad and what is crucial to you. It is probably as easy as analyzing or taking your dog for a stroll. Once you've were given your list of most essential topics, commit time to doing what makes you satisfied every day. Schedule it into your calendar like a meeting in case you need to. Your desires and what you rate the maximum don't trade, so the more you are pronouncing positive to different topics, the extra annoying your existence can be. When someone asks you to perform a little factor that takes time faraway from your important listing, with courtesy tell them you've got already got plans and stick with the ones plans.

three. Make super human beings apprehend your limits in advance than viable invites, just so they're not caught off-protect.

If your week is tiring and you're generally exhausted through Friday middle of the night, make it smooth in your pals that you want the break day and gained't be going out on Friday nights. Making this recognized and sticking in your weapons way they received't even ask you, and you gained't experience accountable about saying no. Establish a few smooth obstacles and permit the human beings to your existence understand approximately them. We may be discussing barriers in extra intensity within the subsequent financial ruin.

4. Use humor to mention no.

My friend hates swimming. He jokes approximately it along along with his next-door friends, who love their pool. Because of this, they understand he will in no manner obtain an invite to come back back swimming. They've even stopped inviting him, it really is a brilliant element due to the fact they recognize his goals. If you don't like dancing and your buddies are typically asking, decline through developing a funny story out of it to reduce the anxiety. That manner, you're no longer right now saying no, but you're however expressing your disinterest inside the interest in a lighthearted way.

five. Weigh up your quick-time period versus lengthy-time period regrets.

Ask yourself in case you'd alternatively remorse the pain of announcing no for a few moments or regret the ache and resentment of getting said sure for the times, weeks or months it may take to conform with through with that dedication.

6. If you haven't already been considering it, the answer isn't always any.

When your buddy asks you to join their scrapbooking club, meditation institution, yoga circle, or after-art work glad hour, and your response isn't, "Oh, my gosh! I've been considering doing that," this is an instance it's a no or at the least, "permit me suppose it over." Take the time to consider what you simply revel in doing and what ought to supply you happiness. If their request isn't a few aspect that's going to serve you, it's okay to say no.

7. Delay giving a right away solution.

Give your self a 2nd to bear in mind what you're saying sure to and what you may be sacrificing if you made a decision to position a while and electricity into the request. Take a deep breath earlier than answering and fall lower lower back on: "I'll get back to you" or "I want to check my calendar first," so you have time to consider it.

8. Ask yourself the manner you'd revel in if the event or venture have grow to be day after today.

It's smooth to assume that the solution is sure if the occasion or challenge isn't for a few days or maybe weeks because of the reality there's a buffer of time making the request appear ability. Imagine in case you needed to do the issue the following day. Think about how you may enjoy and allow that manual your desire.

nine. Know that pronouncing no to the offer doesn't propose saying no to the friendship.

When you say no, be upbeat, powerful, and loving actually so the man or woman is aware of it's not them you're rejecting. This may be especially beneficial if the person is exceedingly touchy. Saying no lovingly suggests that no matter the truth that you could't fulfill the request, you do care approximately them as a person. It moreover lets in to hold your pounding coronary coronary coronary heart calm. To keep the friendship alive and healthful, amplify your very very very own invitation every so often.

10. If you're in a season of sacrifice, say no, best for now.

If you're going through a time in which it's tough to determine to a few factor new, unique that to the character and go away the door open for connecting at a later stage. An example is probably, "I am consumed by way of format ultimate dates proper now, but while subjects ease up in a few weeks, permit's capture lunch."

eleven. Don't say perhaps whilst you absolutely need to mention no.

Saying probable leaves the character with desire in your presence. Saying, "I'll try to make it," prevents the person from planning for the right type of people. A more thoughtful and kinder solution is a immediately no, so no individual is left with expectant emotions.

12. Let your devices set the limits to your behalf.

Turn off any computerized notifications, so you aren't constantly bombarded with social media or e-mail notifications. Use autoresponders to your emails and trade your voicemail. Set up the "I'm riding" notification in your smartphone, so human beings understand you're not to be had to talk at that second. It is proper to set the ones styles of obstacles and say no to people desiring you all the time. If you compromise and answer your telephone outdoor of place of job hours, humans receives into the addiction of facts you're constantly available and gained't apprehend your location.

13. Voice your solution really.

When you need to say no, it is feasible to be every organisation and kind. Avoid overexplaining why you could't or don't need to do what they're asking. Giving reasons to your solution should possibly reason a few people to mission you or discover a way to paintings round your excuse to get you to meet their goals. No is more than sufficient, so apprehend your answer without feeling responsible. If you enjoy like no is genuinely too harsh, strive pronouncing:

• "Unfortunately, that's truely not a few thing I can cope with right now."

• "I'm sorry, but that's no longer going to artwork for me."

• "That appears like amusing, but I received't be available nowadays."

14. Reflect.

This consists of noticing some different individual's emotions and reflecting them returned to them. It might be clearly what they need and does not necessarily advise you're doing the method for them. For example, in case your colleague is continuously asking you for favors, don't supply in to doing them however as an opportunity say a few trouble like, "You appear harassed out nowadays. Is everything ok?" Opening the door for them to vent would likely find the motive they've been the usage of you. Helping them cope with their feelings will motive them to revel in a whole lot extra cared for and heard than in case you have been to truly say positive to their requests. If they even though need assist, having that verbal exchange with them will give you deeper notion into what have to genuinely be useful to them.

15. Be open and honest.

Being open collectively with your friends and own family approximately your need to mention no can be very powerful. Often as HSPs, we keep away from being obvious with others out of worry of rejection or hurting their emotions. However, your friends and circle of relatives will respect it hundreds more if you are sincere and open with them about your desires and limitations. That manner, they don't have to play the guessing hobby, and you don't bottle up any resentment in the route of them.

HOW TO SAY NO WITHOUT FEELING GUILTY

It is probably all properly and properly to practice announcing no, but how do you save you that pang of guilt you enjoy to your heart? As an HSP, we are so in tune with different people's desires and emotions that it can be tough to stick to our barriers and say no without guilt. It may be specially tough to keep away from guilt with reference to saying no to those who are near you. At the forestall of the day, it boils all the manner all the way down to putting your self first and understanding which you want to be located first. Having a sturdy experience of what you want and understanding that you can't serve others with out serving yourself first is a large a part of what softens the guilt. As fairly touchy people, I accept as true with we will normally experience a few shape of guilt at the same time as pronouncing no; it's part of who we are. It indicates that we care—certainly so long as the guilt isn't overwhelming and reasons us disappointed or to offer in and say sure. Here are some one-of-a-kind methods to lessen the guilt while announcing no:

1. Tune in.

Take the time to test in with your self. There is probably times at the same time as you feel together with you need to reply at once but don't forget, you're allowed to ask for time to answer. Ask your self how pronouncing nice or no feels on your body. Tune in in your frame and word in which on your body you feel the emotion and what your frame has to say approximately it. Is it a terrible or extraordinary reaction? As an HSP, you have to continually believe your intestine. As you exercising tuning in and taking note of your dreams, it turns into less difficult to get right of access in your intestine feeling and say no without guilt. Being privy to how your frame feels in any given situation will assist you discover antique styles and behavior that not serve you.

2. Know that it's sincerely now not right for you.

Often as HSPs, we enjoy our answer. Yet, we get stuck in a experience of guilt if we don't do what others ask parents. In the ones moments, it's miles essential to do not forget that sacrificing your very personal goals does not serve anyone. It simplest makes you an awful lot less powerful at helping them. It would in all likelihood experience like pushing your personal desires apart is helping the opposite character, but you're simplest harming your self and the relationship because you're not open and honest. Humans increase thru difficult instances, so in case you're protective a person else's wishes, you could sincerely be stopping them from experiencing an essential lesson they need to go through to increase. Remind your self that during case you're pronouncing certain while you want to say no, you're now not sincerely assisting all people. You may be capable of assist extra human beings when you address your self first.

3. Rephrase your answer.

Sometimes, you can want to say sure, however with a scenario or boundary in location. So, inform the person that, but hold in thoughts that humans reply better to: "Yes, as quick as . . ." than "No, I can't . . ." Saying certain but with a state of affairs in location lets in you to give in on your being concerned and generous nature while nonetheless maintaining a few wholesome barriers so that you have some time for your self and those don't take advantage of you.

Here are a few examples of announcing sure even as despite the fact that having your limits in location:

• "Yes, I assist you to. This week acquired't paintings for me, but I allow you to next week."

• "Sure, I'd need to peer you, so I'll come, but I'm clearly letting I'll want to go away early."

• "I can address the state-of-the-art undertaking, however I will only be capable of perform that at the surrender of the month as quickly as I've completed my present time limits."

four. Express gratitude.

Show yourself some appreciation for those instances you manipulate to paste to your barriers. If saying no has been an extended conflict for you, fame up for yourself can be a profound enjoy. Show yourself a few love and absorb the feeling of empowerment. When falling quick and saying yes without wanting to, show yourself compassion. Likewise, expressing gratitude to the those who recognize your dreams is empowering. It's smooth to anticipate humans want to act a sure manner that would advocate taking the those who do honor your obstacles with no consideration. A smooth "Thank you for being so knowledge" or "That wasn't smooth for me, so I understand which you . . ." can bypass an prolonged manner in putting in healthful, intimate relationships. It in reality reinforces your courting dynamic, making the opposite individual much more likely to appreciate your limits over again inside the future.

For many HSPs, getting to know to mention no with out feeling first rate guilt can take time. However, it may furthermore be deeply recuperation. We want to be compassionate and patient with ourselves throughout the approach of growing and developing greater wholesome conduct.

Chapter 8: The Buck Stops Here

The phrase boundary is described as a few component that marks a border, whether or no longer it is a real or imaginary line that shows the restrict or component. In our non-public lives, boundaries are wholesome and vital for our self-care. Without proper boundaries in place, we're capable of turn out to be feeling depleted, taken as a right, taken benefit of, or encroached upon. Boundaries are there to useful useful resource us in searching after ourselves. They provide us the permission (no longer that we want it, however they permit us) to say no to something that doesn't actually serve us. Boundaries are there to attract a clean line around what's suitable and what is not. They are critical for developing keep in mind and building healthy relationships. Even if someone doesn't similar to the reality that you've said no, they'll despite the fact that possibly respect you for status up for what you want and what you be given as actual with in.

HSPS AND BOUNDARIES

Setting boundaries changed into as soon as exceedingly tough for me, and I continuously ended up on the opposite issue of them. I ended up doing matters in existence I became now not obsessed with in lifestyles—clearly to pride others. At paintings, I might take delivery of obligations which have been pushed onto me although they weren't mine. In my personal existence, I stored quiet in my relationships and in no manner did what I desired to do till anger and resentment defined me and my moves.

It have become most effective as soon as I in the end stopped to do a little deep soul-looking art work that I discovered out I felt intruded upon psychologically, mentally, emotionally, and bodily. I grow to be continuously being asked to perform despite the fact that I changed into without a doubt overwhelmed, and the worst element have come to be that I changed into ultimately the offender. By in no way voicing my limits and setting my limitations in location, I allowed extraordinary human beings to apply me while setting my very non-public highbrow fitness and fulfillment on hold to help them gather their dreams.

I needed to draw that invisible line inside the sand to start protecting myself, my dreams, and my dreams. At first, I felt liable for letting distinct human beings down, and I involved I need to offend people. But then I began operating towards saying "no" with no longer whatever else behind it—no different excuses or reasons. I taught myself that no grow to be an entire sentence, and, inside the beginning, it threw a few human beings off, but I stood sturdy in my want for boundaries in my life.

Children who are quite touchy have an acute enjoy of recognition of the subtle changes within the humans around them, particularly with the adults in their life, like mother and father and teachers. The stop end end result is that most particularly touchy children start adjusting their conduct to ensure others are at ease because they select up on any little shift in precise humans's mood, strength, or body language. Although the purpose behind this is herbal and is a part of what makes us as HSPs so specific, it ends in us struggling with barriers due to the fact we're so sensitive to the subtle modifications in others.

Even even though HSPs are exceptionally compassionate concerning the desires of others, we often forget our very non-public desires. Setting boundaries is tough for us because, as noted within the preceding bankruptcy, we warfare with the word no. We are continuously worried that sticking to our obstacles will harm unique humans's emotions or result in warfare and rejection.

How not placing limitations manifests on your existence

As an HSP, it might experience which consist of you're doing ok. You would possibly have come upon the need for obstacles on a blog put up or Facebook quiz and characteristic a difficult draft of your limits stuffed somewhere on your handbag, but are you genuinely sticking to them? You may revel in such as you've got all of it beneath control and announcing certain to at least one more task may be quality, so long as absolutely all and sundry is happy. I've been on your role, and in my observation, proper right right here is how now not sticking for your obstacles creates problems for an HSP and manifests on your existence:

1. You are always incredible responsible.

You take responsibility for responsibilities that aren't even yours to tackle. As an HSP, you experience what one of a kind people are feeling and realize what they want, and it's ingrained on your nature to want to help them. You won't experience like you can say no, so you say sure. You revel in an duty to help others after they're having a tough time. Guilt drives you to overstep your barriers due to the fact you are worried about what precise people recall you.

2. You are afraid to rock the boat on your relationships.

You continually show kindness and compassion and supply someone the benefit of the doubt within the event that they've had a tough day. You usually need your relationships to be on top notch terms, so you are commonly eager to delight. Whenever your associate or friends ask you what's incorrect, you brush it off and inform them the whole thing is best, even if you're irritated or inexperienced with envy. The idea of voicing your critiques or desires leaves you feeling flustered. You are involved which you'll cry because of the fact you're indignant, otherwise you'll get embarrassed and forget what you've got been attempting to mention.

3. You sacrifice your private properly-being.

Self-care is the last element in your list, and that's if it's even made it to the listing the least bit. Saying no and sticking for your limitations to get a few relaxation doesn't appear like a valid reason. You are afraid you'll be visible as too sensitive or inclined in case you tell human beings you are exhausted. Trying to reveal you're always able to being treasured results in you announcing positive to subjects that aren't first-rate for you. It consequences in you seeking to bear some thing you've taken on despite the reality that your health is taking a toll. You've turn out to be so aware about setting the desires of numerous human beings first that you don't simply recognize what you want or need anymore.

four. People continuously stroll at some point of you.

You have a tough time retaining people liable for their moves. It's tough so you can follow through together with your pals, family, employees, or maybe clients once they miss a cut-off date or don't comply with through on some component they said they'll do. When a person does some thing wrong, you restore it in place of confronting them approximately it, because of this they never studies the effects and don't positioned in the attempt due to the fact they understand you'll be there to easy up any mess. You permit people break out with stuff due to the fact you don't need to make them disillusioned or irritated, due to this you are making it acknowledged that your emotions are a bargain much less essential than theirs.

Why you want obstacles as an HSP

Everyone needs to have obstacles, however they may be in particular vital for rather sensitive humans because of the truth we are so strongly stricken by one-of-a-kind humans and our surroundings. Boundaries are a manner for us to filter what we will and can't do. They permit in what we will deal with and hold out the topics that exhaust, crush, or damage us.

In every dating we've got were given, there may be an energy trade. When we interact with one of a type human beings, there are connections at play: the connection to ourselves and our reference to them. Because of our perceptiveness as HSPs, we realize what the possibility individual desires, so it feels herbal to place them within the spotlight. We can also revel in the need to hold a pleasant connection to them, even though it technique sacrificing our connection to ourselves and what's essential to us. We need to have limitations as HSPs because of the fact if our wishes go with the flow unacknowledged, we'll turn out to be feeling depleted and resentful. It is feasible for 2 humans to percent the highlight.

Without limitations, it's too quick and clean to mention certain with out definitely thinking about what the venture includes. Having obstacles gives us the buffer we want to have a "track-in" 2nd wherein we make the aware decision now not to tackle a few other person's mind, feelings, or strength. Tuning in to ourselves is so essential as it offers us a 2nd to invite ourselves what we want. It may be as simple as developing a grocery list of all of the assets you need to get that your family enjoys and then taking a 2d to encompass the stuff you want on the list as properly.

Boundaries are basically the limits we need to set to defend ourselves. Boundaries are there to defend us from bodily damage, the burn-out that carries overcommitting, or the pain of being round someone with excessive or horrific energy. Boundaries are there to defend our active space. They are a way to enhance our instinct and better apprehend how to take care of our desires.

Boundaries you want to set as an HSP

As HSPs, we can't allow our very own fears or what society says dictate who we are. Our lives are in our palms, and we get to pick wherein we skip, who we hold out with, and what we tackle. Setting wholesome limits will help us get up for ourselves in all elements of our lives, and the following are some areas to recall placing barriers:

1. Living environment.

Our at once residing and paintings environments are truely crucial. Most HSPs need matters to be efficient and prepared. Clutter or chaos in our homes or on our desks throws us off direction. The right information is that we've got were given a say in how topics want to be finished. Of direction, it's masses much less hard in case you live on my own or earn a living from home, however even then, there are still humans to do not forget. An important boundary to set for your living surroundings is to permit humans understand how vital it is on your nicely-being to have your subjects stay orderly. Ask the humans concerned to each assist out or at least appreciate the guidelines you have to your space.

2. Crowd control.

It's no longer continuously possible to interrupt out a crowd, so it's vital to understand a way to live on while we're in a unmarried. Just like a superhero has a bent to have their healthy beneath their garments, we want to do the same thing. Except in area of suits, your superpower is your excessive sensitivity. As an HSP, it's time to personal the power you have got have been given and not run away from it. You need to forestall seeking to be regular and encompass who you're. When you're in a crowd, you may stand enterprise, lean in, and pay attention to the cries of humans in want. However, the trick is to use discernment. You are not liable for saving absolutely everyone, and masses of people don't need to be saved anyway. They need to experience visible and heard. Choose who you're inclined to renowned in a crowd, and don't worry about the rest. Your notably touchy abilties and stressful nature may simply be the mild someone needs on that day.

three. Takers.

There are many takers on this worldwide, and that they will be predisposed to gravitate closer to HSPs due to the reality we're natural givers. We need to set limitations for while we're round individuals who best need a few thing from us. It is important for our fitness. If you're in a crowd like in the above factor and encounter a taker, it's far essential to maintain in mind it isn't your mission to keep people and widely recognized you have got got nothing to provide them.

four. Food and liquids.

The pronouncing "you are what you eat" is real. As HSPs, our our our bodies don't outstanding absorb the vitamins or the pollutants inside the meals we devour however take within the food's strength as nicely. You may also additionally find out that some meals have power that virtually doesn't take delivery of as real along with your body. We need to create barriers around meals and beverages that don't depart us feeling fantastic and not revel in pressured into indulging without a doubt because of the reality everybody else is doing it.

five. Relationships.

This is one region we, as HSPs, definitely need barriers. We enjoy the feelings of others as despite the fact that they have been our personal, and we don't want the human beings in our lives to enjoy ache, so we supply ourselves over to every whim of our children or companions. However, this is not a sustainable way to stay. We become overwhelmed and exhausted and retreat or retaliate in risky methods. We keep at once to resentment because of the reality we experience our goals are unimportant, but we try this to ourselves. This can create a in reality uncomfortable duality in our minds. Happy and healthy relationships need easy barriers. Setting limits starts with understanding your values. When you experience crushed, it's far normally because definitely considered one in every of your values is compromised. From your values, you may set healing barriers to be able to gain you and the relationships on your life.

6. Television and technology.

Television and generation are every gear used for connection, but they can also negatively have an effect on our health. Watching a movie is a incredible way to wind down and spend time with your partner, but if the movie is violent, you're probable going to experience simply uncomfortable as a substitute of having a dopamine hit. The equal may be said for generation. Our laptops and telephones positioned the sector at our fingertips, however if we spend all our time hiding in the back of them, we're going to overlook out at the real connections with the human beings we are trying to find. Setting barriers with technology and the TV can be important in your fitness.

7. Time management.

Where hobby is going, power flows. The way we manage our hobby will impact how we spend our time. We need to set limitations spherical what we awareness our interest on during the day. Having an if/then protocol in place truely helped me manipulate my interest and time. An instance of this might be, "If I am tempted to scroll via Instagram on the same time as I am writing a weblog, then I will upward push up and get a tumbler of water to drink earlier than sitting back down to art work."

Having if/whilst protocols in vicinity can help us make the crucial alternatives to stay heading in the right direction with our intentions.

Examples of obstacles

Here are some examples of limitations you can set that prioritize your dreams:

• Telling your boss that, regrettably, you acquired't be able to art work past due.

• Requesting that a person else trade their behavior in region of you being the only to compromise.

• Declining an invitation or request for help from a person.

• Asking a grandparent no longer to provide your children cookies or candy before time for supper.

• Limiting your self to 1 glass of wine.

• Leaving the room whilst a person makes you uncomfortable in any other case you select up horrible electricity.

• Telling your co-worker which you discover their jokes or foul language offensive and which you'd like them to save you.

• Hanging up the mobile phone while someone is shouting at you.

- Turning your cellphone off at an less expensive hour to avoid being woken up via past due-night time notifications.

- Not answering your smartphone or e mail after artwork hours.

- Creating a meditation exercise that you could use to protect your strength.

- Knowing it's proper to inform your friends you don't experience like going out for beverages after artwork.

- Creating the space you want among you and friends or circle of relatives who you discover draining.

- Not answering calls or texts that call for energy at the same time as you're feeling exhausted.

HOW TO START SETTING BOUNDARIES

People always communicate about limitations as although they will be clean to installation, and anyone respects them. However, if you're an HSP who has in no manner in reality had limits or barriers, that may be less difficult stated than done. Fortunately, there are techniques to discover ways to set boundaries so you can start placing yourself first. Learning to set limits doesn't appear in a day, every week, or even a month, however the extra you exercise, the less complex it will become.

1. Start small.

Don't try to make each alternate and set too many barriers all at the same time. Give yourself the time to ease into your boundary-placing goals. Make a listing of the boundaries you want to put in vicinity, and start with the smaller ones. As you gain more self perception, you'll be capable of flow directly to the more difficult boundaries.

2. Slow down.

When it comes time to decide what you need to mention sure to, you'll probable feel forced to answer immediately. However, except it's miles an emergency, you don't need to reply at that second. Slow down and take as a whole lot time as you need to carefully keep in mind the request or invitation in advance than committing to it. It's truly good enough to say, "I need to think about it, and I'll will let you recognize." Taking some time earlier than figuring out will assist you take a look at whether or not or now not the request crosses a boundary, and if it does, you will be a great deal much less in all likelihood to enjoy accountable while declining.

3. Give yourself permission.

Our emotions of guilt, worry, and self-doubt often prevent us from expressing our dreams and voicing our opinions. As HSPs, we fear approximately how specific human beings will react to our requests—this is considered one of the largest hurdles we are coping with even as placing wholesome limitations. One element that would notably help you in masses of factors of your existence is giving yourself permission to do what you want to do. The fact is that we will be predisposed to live up for special humans to present us permission or inform us it's adequate to speak up about our goals. However, the duty to speak our desires have to completely be on us due to the fact no man or woman else truely knows what we need; best we do. So, offer your self permission to set boundaries and limitations. Know that you are only accountable for your very personal movements and aren't accountable for the moves of various human beings.

4. Focus on setting boundaries respectfully and now not seeking to manipulate how fantastic people respond.

While it's real to preserve in mind the feelings and desires of others, it is also critical to undergo in mind that we can't manage how exclusive humans react. For instance, sincerely due to the fact you're well mannered doesn't recommend someone received't yell at you. It is likewise crucial to preserve in mind that not the whole lot is about you. Often human beings may additionally lash out at you or appear angry while you implement your boundary, however there's a extremely good chance that some component else has contributed to their feelings and actions. Other human beings's goals are not extra essential than yours, and it's not selfish to take care of yourself first.

5. Ask yourself a few questions.

I discover it pretty beneficial to magazine at the questions underneath. Seeing the terms on paper creates even deeper clarity and makes limitations less hard to set:

• What limitations do I want to put in region for me to live in my integrity?

• Am I burdening myself with the strength and troubles of various people that aren't mine to preserve?

• What might likely my work surroundings and personal life appear like if I took on a good buy much less, blamed myself a exquisite deal less, and had greater understand for my very non-public obstacles?

• What moves, obligations, situations, behaviors, or people am I tolerating which may be draining me?

PUTTING YOUR BOUNDARIES INTO PLACE

Knowing the manner to start setting boundaries is step one, but the subsequent step is to place them into location and start running within the course of. Sticking in your limits will gain your regular well-being, intellectual fitness, coronary coronary heart, and bodily health. When you start saying no to three component that doesn't serve you and fine to what you need to do, you'll find out that you will be happier, greater healthful, and extra assured.

1. Know your self and gather your limits.

Being self-aware will help you are making alternatives that certainly serve you. I am a essentially introverted HSP. Although many advantages include these traits, there are also some boundaries. For instance, you could recognize that your hobby wherein you spend eight hours in an place of business with noisy people is draining, so going out after paintings to socialize isn't always as fun or a laugh because it might be for distinctive people. You recognize that you want by myself time so that you can placed into impact obstacles that create and guard that factor. Everyone will have tremendous limits, however none people have limitless quantities of time and strength. We want to create barriers, so we don't overgive, overcommit, and overexert ourselves.

2. Identify what's essential to you and determine to defend that aspect.

It's going to be problematic on the way to set boundaries in case you aren't positive what your need and dreams are. It is important to recognize what feels proper and what feels incorrect. Begin via compiling a list of what you cost and preserve close to your heart. Write down the manner you need to be dealt with with the aid of the usage of manner of various people. You can use the list of what's crucial to you and your values to recognise even as someone is overstepping virtually one in every of your barriers. You'll have the ability to talk greater assertively and in reality due to the fact you apprehend what you will tolerate and what not.

3. Pay hobby to the way you enjoy and what you want.

Your gut feeling, physical sensations, mind, and emotions are all suitable signs and symptoms of on the equal time as you need to set barriers. Tune in in your feelings at some level inside the day and make an effort to assess what you want at that second.

four. Make your limits identified.

Make splendid the people in your lifestyles are aware about your limits earlier than they invite you somewhere or ask you to perform a little aspect, in order that they're not amazed when you decline.

5. Pay interest to at the identical time as you enjoy triggered through unique humans.

Generally, humans are interested by the maximum effective strength in the room and align themselves with that character. As an HSP, it is essential to be privy to even as this is taking region and which man or woman it has a bent to expose up throughout the maximum. By noticing this, you will be capable of live right to your actual, touchy nature at the equal time as final strong and inner your barriers.

6. Notice in which and while you feel the most beaten.

As an HSP, you usually recognise what influences you the maximum, but it is vital to check in with your self often to be aware of what might be taking place for you. Pay unique interest to the sports you attend, the interactions you have got were given, and the responsibilities that depart you feeling overwhelmed and exhausted. Becoming aware of your intellectual and emotional state is step one to knowledge your private power. It will help you get clean on any adjustments you'd want to make or limitations you need to set to preserve your very very own private peace.

7. Me/not-me idea of obstacles.

The me/now not-me approach lets in you outline your non-public lively and private region. It permits you claim what isn't yours.

Practicing me/now not-me will help you enjoy more constant, safe, and strong in almost each situation. With exercise, you may start noticing on the same time as one of a kind humans's mind and feelings are affecting you far more rapid, which makes it less tough to release with plenty much less try. Here is a easy me/now not-me exercise to you get you started out:

• Stand or sit in a stable, quiet area in which you're by myself and near your eyes.

• Say your call to yourself. Feel the essence of who you're even as you are saying it. Tune in to the sensation of being your real self.

• Imagine a circle of slight spherical you; it can be any shade and may increase or 3 feet outward in all instructions. This mild serves as your lively boundary. Declare to the universe and yourself that that vicinity is yours and no man or woman else's. Anything that isn't-me isn't allowed inside the vicinity and desires to live outside the boundary circle.

- Say your call all over again and easy out something that is not-me from your private area. You can remember it leaving your circle in any way you choice. I for my part want to assume that a few aspect no longer-me leaves in the shape of gray smoke blowing away.

- When you're out in a crowd or round special people, frequently declare your me/no longer-me with the useful resource of acting this workout and visualizing your active boundary. Visualize that other people's energies jump off your space. You can meet their feelings, mind, and emotions with know-how and compassion out at the threshold of your boundary in your creativeness, however their power isn't allowed access into your location!

ENFORCING YOUR BOUNDARIES

There is not any element in doing all of the art work to set up your boundaries in case you don't maintain and put into effect them. Here are a few approaches you may growth your limitations and purpose them to paste:

1. Be direct.

Asking for what you need or saying "no" can be intimidating. However, with the resource of asking right now and actually for what you need or desire, you're much more likely to be understood and characteristic your dreams met. Saying "possibly" or "I'm not powerful" whilst you really need to mention "no" will simplest confuse different humans and may bring about them feeling indignant or crushed. When you've located a boundary in place, it is fine to express it certainly and without delay.

2. Express gratitude.

Show yourself some appreciation for the instances you have were given got efficaciously set and fixed for your barriers. If you've struggled with this for a long time, popularity up for your self can be profound and empowering. In the times which you fall brief, display yourself compassion. It is also empowering to reveal gratitude to the humans that recognize your obstacles.

three. Be inclined to interrupt the social settlement.

To defend and placed into impact your limitations, you have to be inclined to brush aside or ruin the social agreement. Simply positioned, the social agreement is the set of unwritten suggestions that govern our social interactions. For example, getting up and leaving mid-conversation with out a word is in opposition to the social settlement. It can be seen as impolite and bizarre. Another instance is walking as much as a stranger and placing your hand on them. Generally, folks who smash the social agreement are seen as extraordinary, have low emotional intelligence and are poorly calibrated. However, the social agreement is also a way that some people advantage have an effect on over others. One of the most obvious techniques that is finished is thru the guideline of thumb of reciprocation—if someone is visible as doing a choice for you, you must sense a experience of duty to repay them with a decide upon. There may be times even as it's essential to push aside or damage the social agreement to keep your barriers intact and guard your vicinity.

4. Have effects in location.

Always pick out a consequence you can with out trouble observe via on. Setting barriers permits to permit the opposite individual recognize what will appear in the event that they don't recognize them. Be as specific and sensible as feasible. Don't set repercussions which is probably vague or out of percentage to the boundary being violated. For example, you may say, "Dad, I've informed you I don't like it when you touch upon my weight. If you hold doing that, I'm going to head home."

five. Be regular together along with your limitations.

If you're inconsistent together collectively with your limitations, you can turn out to be complicated human beings. If you don't stick with your boundaries, a few human beings will take opportunities and move them. Once you placed a boundary, do your awesome to put into effect it and constantly perform the consequences you've stated.

6. Stand your ground if someone resists.

People is probably irritated or disenchanted along with your new limitations on the begin. The humans to your existence may additionally additionally take it in my opinion while you set a boundary with them. They may also even intentionally push your obstacles to appearance what they could escape with. If a person does this, lightly and firmly remind them of your limits and the consequences within the occasion that they don't apprehend them.

7. Reassure your family if they will be feeling damage.

Explain that the bounds you're setting aren't supposed to be hurtful or disenchanted them. Setting barriers with human beings you care about can be difficult. If your beloved's feelings are damage, make the effort to remind them that you care about them and that your limitations are there to help your relationships, no longer harm them.

CREATING YOUR OWN COMFORT ZONE

As alternatively sensitive people, our out of doors environments considerably have an effect on our inner lives. We enjoy the whole lot so deeply. Our highs are very joyous, and our lows gift demanding conditions that have an effect on our capacity to control. Each and every day comes with a sensory overload which could depart us with strong emotions that, if left unchecked, have a terrible impact on our intellectual health and first-rate of life. That is why, as HSPs, we need to create a consolation region for ourselves—a sanctuary in which we're able to go to recharge. It is essential to boom systems and practices that lets in you to help us shield ourselves from out of doors factors that may be overwhelming.

BECOMING AWARE OF YOUR EMOTIONS

As an HSP, I find out myself suffering with the hassle of being rational. The definition of rational is "primarily based totally on information or cause and not on feelings or emotions." It is a idea method that employs purpose, logical and systematic techniques to obtain a end or remedy a hassle. I don't recognise about you, but that is not how my mind works. That's now not how maximum particularly touchy people address troubles. Instead, if there may be a hassle, we spend a big amount of time wallowing inside the feeling the hassle inspires. We are at risk of preserving at once to our emotions at the same time as looking for an answer, which clouds our attitude in desire to viewing the problem objectively.

There is certainly no longer a few element incorrect with that way of processing. However, the threat takes vicinity at the same time as we lose ourselves in our emotions and don't really remedy the hassle. I realise that I've been there, blinded with emotion and glued with out an get away. This can result in a downward spiral of awful thoughts, despair, and anxiety.

It is so important for us to turn out to be aware about our feelings and recognize what we're feeling and why the ones feelings are there. When we aren't privy to our emotions, it is not going we'll determine out a way to alter them. When we become privy to our emotions, they may be able to't manipulate us as masses.

You might be thinking, "How is it feasible that I'm now not privy to my emotions? I am the one who feels the whole lot so deeply ultimately." Although that is actual, we're able to enjoy a few aspect deeply however although no longer be aware about the fact that we're feeling a few detail.

Sometimes our feelings can also power us to do some component we didn't want to do (like pronouncing positive or lashing out), and in a while, we feel green with envy, shameful, or responsible. This whole state of affairs is complicated and may reason pretty some confusion internal us. In some instances, our confusion would possibly likely end up so sturdy that it becomes the trouble itself, and this is while rationality wants to kick in.

When you locate yourself suffering with terrible mind that you actually can't overcome, take a step once more and ask yourself, what's sincerely happening? Take a second to evaluate the situation and what you're going thru. Then ask yourself, how do I sense at this second? Is it worry? Anger? Sadness? If not, what is it? This is each other great possibility to capture your mag and free write it out.

Once you may pinpoint exactly what's bothering your mind, you switch out to be privy to its presence, and then you definitely have two alternatives: you could allow or not it's, or you can do a little component to create exchange.

Meet your emotions

When sturdy feelings upward push up in us HSPs, it is able to revel in like a bodily sensation bubbling up interior. Depending at the scenario, we juggle handling ourselves with calm compassion or letting our emotions explode. Naturally, the latter can be messy. It is inside the ones moments of explosion that the humans spherical us name us overly touchy. After all, we allow our feelings get the better humans, which might be hurtful within the course of ourselves and others.

This truly does no longer suggest we need to bottle up our feelings and desire they'll leave on their very very own. Pushing feelings aside is some thing that many HSPs do, mainly once they've been reprimanded for expressing their feelings.

Instead, we need to put in force a clean procedure that begins with acknowledging that we are feeling some thing and that some thing has the proper to speak with us. We want to start assembly our emotions, and a splendid area to start is with this little exercising this is similar to how we meet people.

Start with the beneficial aid of saying, "My call is (insert your call). What's your name?" Then don't forget the emotion replying, "Hello (your name). I'm sadness combined with a touch rejection." Labeling your emotion as specifically as you could is the first step towards overcoming and releasing it.

Another workout is to clearly pick out wherein the emotion is most lively in our bodies. Often, hastily while we discover in which the emotion is positioned, its intensity will reduce without us actively doing a little aspect. In this way, our feelings are like dogs who want our attention. The emotions want to be cited. Once we apprehend them, they may be an entire lot a good deal much less possibly to rebel and purpose us to explode.

Ask your self a few important questions

Once you're familiar with the emotion you're feeling, you need to ask your self some important questions. After turning into acquainted with the emotion hiding inside the back of your moves, it's miles essential to investigate it to the exceptional of your capability. The crucial element is to be completely sincere with your self even as answering them. It will take some time to discover ways to be apparent with yourself and others, but it's now not now not viable. Once once more, that is an extraordinary time to put your pen to paper. Writing topics out is an extra shape of remedy and release whilst addressing feelings.

- Why do I enjoy this way?

- What evoked this feel interior me?

- Has this sense me earlier than?

- Do I want to enjoy this manner? Do I need to?

- Am I specializing in judging myself in region of information and empathizing?

- Am I in particular compelled or burnt out proper now?

- Did I get sufficient sleep? Did I devour?

- Am I outside my ordinary or comfort place?

- How can I compassionately decide myself proper now?

Once you've diagnosed the emotion and what added on it, it could now not manage you into doing a little issue you don't need to do, and it now not has such power over you.

HAVE A PLAN TO PROTECT YOURSELF

As an HSP, it is important to discover ways to address existence's stresses. Most of our pressure comes from out of doors stimuli and from being overwhelmed. It is crucial to have a plan to manage in stressful environments and placed into effect a barrier among us and any overpowering sensory stimuli.

Here are some techniques to protect yourself as an HSP:

• Add positivity on your existence via incorporating activities you experience to stability out any extra strain you can come upon. Take the time to do the topics that make you satisfied.

• Avoid any stressors or triggers like violent films or individuals who make you sense terrible about your self. Stay smooth from any environments wherein human beings drain your power or make heavy needs of you.

• Apply what we included in Chapter 4, study to mention no to any overwhelming requests, and don't feel lousy approximately it. Create and positioned into effect obstacles on your life that make pronouncing no much less difficult.

• Set up a safe area in which you could flow into and recharge. Make your home a secure region with a chilled environment—a sanctuary wherein you could destress.

• At art work, leave an opening amongst your appointments to permit your self a danger to decompress. Have set hours at the same time as your colleagues can drop with the aid of or implement a boundary wherein you time table appointments to avoid random interruptions that spike your pressure.

• Implement an 80/20 rule. Always give up whilst you're earlier in phrases of your strength. I cannot strain this enough. HSPs frequently sense tired and feeling burnt out is their ordinary. Feeling properly and keeping this sense may be overseas to you within the beginning, but it's far normal and essential. Never allow your self get so overstimulated thru one venture that it affects your capability to do the whole thing else you want to do. Stop—rest—recharge while you acquire eighty% stimulation.

• When using social media, installation your debts to incredible look at customers that positioned up content material cloth that without a doubt have an effect on you. Unfollow any payments that make you feel horrible approximately your self. Don't aimlessly scroll via your social media feeds. Open the app with a cause and when you're completed, near it over again to keep away from mindlessly scrolling. Turning off notifications is likewise splendidly empowering.

• Stop the glorification of being busy. Society glorifies being busy. We're made to sense that if we're not continuously walking spherical doing matters, we're no longer efficient. HSPs want greater downtime than special people to recharge. If you're continuously on the bypass and continuously careworn and frazzled, you need to reevaluate and gradual down.

• Most especially sensitive people love books, so healthy in time to observe a bit bit every day. Reading is the form of downtime HSPs want that soothes and informs.

DEALING WITH NON-HSPS

1. Accept that non-HSPs obtained't understand you.

Many human beings don't recognize HSPs, and we're continuously being informed to stop being touchy or simply recover from it, even into our person lives. The truth that human beings don't feel the way we do or understand why we enjoy the manner we do can go away us feeling like something is incorrect with us. We want to just accept that wonderful people aren't going to recognize us, and it's k.

2. Collaborate with non-HSPs.

Sometimes taking aspect with someone who's non-HSP and extroverted can be a superb partnership. Their huge manner of viewing the arena and the rate at which they make options complements an HSPs slower and deeper technique. A partnership amongst a non-HSP and an HSP will provide unique views and power to the undertaking.

three. Communicate in reality.

Clearly and proper away speaking your need and goals will more than probable come as a extremely good comfort to non-HSPs, specially in the event that they're a cherished one. As an HSP, it may be hard to speak successfully even as you're going via an internal typhoon. But at those times, strolling via the 'meet your emotion workout' may be beneficial. Once you recognize what you're feeling in greater detail, it'll be much less complicated to speak with others.

ADVOCATE FOR YOURSELF

As an HSP, you could on occasion experience collectively with you've misplaced manage over your existence, rights, and responsibilities. Advocating for yourself will assist you regain your feel of manipulate and supply once more the self guarantee and shallowness you want to artwork closer to living a happier lifestyles.

Here are some approaches to endorse for your self:

1. Educate others.

You don't always want to inform anybody you meet which you're an HSP, but make sure those human beings crucial to you understand. Clearly talk your goals and limitations on your family, friends, and pals. Educating distinct human beings about the manner you characteristic as an HSP will assist them recognize your behaviors and the way they could excellent useful resource you.

2. Believe in yourself.

This is less complicated said than completed however consider in yourself and learn how to love the fact which you're highly touchy. Although being an HSP might also moreover have a few drawbacks, you may learn to address the ones. However, being an HSP furthermore has many outstanding capabilities that exclusive humans don't have, so have an extremely good time them and take transport of your self for who you are.

3. Know your needs.

By facts your wishes, you may be able to placed boundaries in region to guard your self and make certain your desires are met. If you don't apprehend what you need, it will likely be a good buy less complex for humans to push you round and take advantage of your giving nature.

four. Have strategies in place.

Make a list of what you'll say to 1-of-a-kind people in situations in that you need to mention no and practice it. Know the manner you'll stay with your barriers. Have strategies in location that sell your properly-being.

five. Communicate and specific yourself firmly and truely.

When you're pronouncing no, you don't want to offer a whole clarification behind your answer. When humans push you, exercise placing forward yourself and status your ground. If a person attempts to cause with you, repeat yourself and deliver a lift for your boundary. It can be tough to begin with, but you can discover it much less complicated to speak your desires and upward thrust up for your self with workout.

www.ingramcontent.com/pod-product-compliance
Lightning Source LLC
Chambersburg PA
CBHW050407120526
44590CB00015B/1872